ANNELIESE MICHEL

A TRUE STORY OF A CASE OF DEMONIC POSSESSION

GERMANY 1976

Fr. Jose Antonio Fortea
Lawrence E.U. LeBlanc

Anneliese Michel

A true story of a case of demonic possession
Germany - 1976

The true story behind the movies The Exorcism of Emily Rose and
Requiem
Fr. Jose Antonio Fortea
Lawrence E.U. LeBlanc

Text copyright 2012 Jose Antonio Fortea and Lawrence E.U. LeBlanc

All Rights Reserved

"Whatever the less discerning theologians may say, the devil, as far as Christian belief is concerned, is a puzzling but real, personal and not merely symbolic presence. The more one understands the holiness of God, the more one understands the opposite of what is holy, namely the deceptive masks of the devil."
Pope Benedict XVI

"The battle against the devil, which is the principal task of Saint Michael the archangel, is still being fought today, because the devil is still alive and active in the world. The evil that surrounds us today, the disorders that plague society, man's inconsistency and brokenness, are not only the results of original sin, but also the result of Satan's pervasive and dark action."
Pope John Paul II at the Sanctuary of Saint Michael May 24, 1987

"She died to save lost souls, to atone for their sins. Anneliese was a kind, loving, sweet and obedient girl. But when she was possessed, it was something unnatural, something that you cannot explain."
Anna Michel, Anneliese's mother, 2005

On March 30, 1978, the trial began in the district court of Aschaffenburg Germany, of Josef and Anna Michel and Father Arnold Renz and Father Ernst Alt. The four were charged with negligent homicide in the death of Anneliese Michel. The courtroom sitting area was occupied primarily by media persons from Germany and abroad. Anneliese, her family, a few close friends, and the two priests involved and their Bishop, all believed that Anneliese suffered from possession. At the time, it was the first official and public case of exorcism in Germany in approximately fifty years, and the only known case to have been recorded on audio tapes. After sixty-seven exorcism sessions, Anneliese died on July 1, 1976 of what appeared to be starvation.

"The Klingenberg case was for all those involved, a breathtaking experience. Someone on the outside cannot possibly appreciate this experience. Man's imagination is stretched past the limit when it comes to demonic possession."

Father Ernst Alt, exorcist of Anneliese

PART I

CHAPTER I

EARLY YEARS

Anneliese Michel was born in Lieblfing Germany on September 21, 1952 to Anna and Josef Michel, and was baptized the following day. She came from a hardworking, traditional Catholic family. The Michels lived in a comfortable two story house in Klingenberg not far from the sawmill that Josef owned and operated. Anneliese's older sister Martha died at the age of eight from complications during an operation to remove a tumor from her kidney. After Anneliese, Anna gave birth to Gertraud Maria in 1954, Barbara in 1956 and Roswitha Christine in 1957.

Anna was born in 1920. She attended three years of secondary school before completing commercial training. Since Anna spent most of her time working in the business, Anneliese's religious grandmother often looked after the children and helped educate them in their faith. Before she married Josef, Anna lived at home and worked in the office of her father's sawmill.

Standing Anneliese, Barbara, Roswitha, Gertraud, seated Anna and Josef

Josef was born in 1917. He began secondary school in Miltenberg at the age of ten. His mother hoped he would become a priest. Three of her sisters were nuns who taught school. Catholic parents often encouraged one or more of their children to enter the priesthood or religious life. Josef did well in school but struggled with Latin. His mother reluctantly agreed to Josef's changeover to a trade school. At the age of twenty-two he was drafted into the army and fought on the eastern and western fronts. Towards the end of World War II, Josef was taken prisoner by the Americans. He was released in June 1945 and went to Munich to attend school for construction. He successfully completed his master's exam in 1948 and took over the family business in Klingenberg. Josef was the fifth generation Michel in this enterprise. He modernized and expanded the business. In 1950 Josef and Anna were married.

Klingenberg, "Blade Mountain," is a small town overlooking the Main River. On one side of the Main River are the forests of the Odenwald and on the other, the forests of the Spessart. Klingenberg, which belongs to the district of Obernburg in Bavaria, is well known for its vineyards on the town's terraced hills and is about a forty-five minute drive southeast of Frankfurt. Today its population is approximately 6,500.

Although Anneliese's three younger sisters were healthy, Anneliese had little resistance to childhood diseases. Before the age of five she contracted mumps, measles and scarlet fever. As a result, she was held back a year in school. At first Communion, Anneliese was slighter than the other girls but seemed to be outgrowing her health problems.

Anneliese liked to sing and play the accordion and piano. She was a good student. Her teachers and professors always had good things to say about her, and Anna hoped Anneliese would one day become a schoolteacher.

Josef and Anna were strict and protective with their girls. Anna left most of the decision making to Josef. The girls went to church on Sundays with their parents and sometimes on weekday evenings. They often prayed the rosary together at home. The Michels noted the thirteenth day of the month in honor of Our Lady of Fatima. While growing up, the children said their morning prayers, prayers to Saint Joseph, the Blessed Virgin Mary and their guardian angels.

Chapter II

FIRST ENCOUNTERS

During the month of September 1968, around the time of Anneliese's sixteenth birthday, a dramatic change occurred in her life. While sitting next to her friend Marieluise Burdich, Anneliese suddenly lost consciousness. Marieluise was frightened, but as Anneliese quickly recovered, they both had a laugh, not knowing what lay ahead. Anneliese passed this episode off as being overtired. After midnight, something more serious occurred. She woke up and couldn't move. An unknown force pinned her down. It pressed on her stomach and she could feel warm urine wetting her clothing. Her breathing was labored and her tongue was as if paralyzed. She tried to wake her sister in the adjoining bed but was unable to speak. Within minutes, it was over. The pressure was gone. Only her tongue was sore. Terrified and barely able to move, she changed the linen on her bed. In the morning, she was too tired to go to school. Anneliese confided to her mother the events of the night before. She recovered quickly, continued to receive good grades in school and relaxed by playing tennis. As time passed, it was forgotten.

Everything seemed to be going well until almost one year later. During the afternoon of August 24, 1969, Anneliese experienced another brief blackout. Then, late in the evening she experienced a frightening paralysis, during which her arms were completely stiff, and she was unable to breathe or cry out for help. Within minutes, it was over. Anneliese changed and went back to bed.

The next morning, Anneliese and Anna visited their family physician, Dr. Gerhard Vogt. He immediately referred them to the neurologist Dr. Luthy in Aschaffenburg. Dr. Luthy asked many questions and ran a number of tests. He found no concerns from a neurological or psychological perspective. Anneliese and Anna returned on August 27 for an EEG. The EEG showed normal brain activity. Dr. Luthy judged from the description he was given, that this was probably a case of cerebral seizures, with symptoms of grand mal epilepsy. No anticonvulsant drug was prescribed at the time as the seizures were far apart. Anna was concerned about whether her daughter's future plans to become a teacher would be jeopardized and about what others might think.

When Anneliese started back to school after her visit to Dr. Luthy, she was not well. She complained of a sore throat. Her tonsils were removed and she subsequently contracted pleurisy and pneumonia. She had to stop attending school and was confined to bed at home. With no improvement in January, she was admitted to the hospital in Aschaffenburg. On February 28, 1970 Anneliese was moved to a clinic in Mittelberg which specialized in bronchial and lung disease for young people. Shortly after she was admitted, her parents were told that she had heart and circulatory problems.

During her stay in Mittelberg, Anneliese dedicated an increased amount of time to prayer and contemplated what she should do with her life. She debated whether she would continue in Aschaffenburg to become a school teacher, or take courses necessary to become a catechist. After her mother visited her, Anneliese wrote Anna stating:

> "I will try to obtain the Abitur [exams to gain entrance to university] even though before you came, I had come to the resolution, not to pursue the Abitur, but to become a catechist. I can always do that if I don't succeed in obtaining the Abitur. Perhaps I can better use my abilities and talents if I become a teacher. There are no accidents in life. It is all in the providence of God. So I have arranged things with the Mother of God that I will become a catechist if I don't obtain the Abitur, but in the case that I obtain it, I will become a school teacher." [1]

In another letter to Anna, Anneliese wrote:

> "Actually, I am quite glad I have been sick, since one comes to see things. One comes to recognize that there are other values besides money, riches and cars, which are worth living for; that one is on this earth for the glory of God and not for transitory things. You should consider this also sometimes. When one is healthy and is immersed in his daily routine, he thinks, all is well with me, why should I be concerned if others in Biafra or Latin America are starving to death, the important thing is that all is going well with me. What is worse at the present time is the indifference towards our neighbors… People today can be so inhuman because all is going well for them. Really, the horrors of the last war ought to remain imprinted on them. But today that is all forgotten." Later she says "You can mark one thing for sure, I want to go to heaven, cost what it may; to gain heaven, nothing is too much for me…On that account I should place my life at the disposal of others out of love for God, and hope more for the reward of God than for the reward of men. Better to be despised by men than by God. Perhaps you know now why I would like to become a catechist; if God has ordained that for me. And be glad I think that way and that you don't have a street girl for a daughter." [2]

Monika Fichtel roomed with Anneliese for most of her stay in Mittelberg and remembered Anneliese as a happy person with a positive outlook on life. She was religious and didn't talk about her health concerns. In later correspondence with Monika, Anneliese often brought up religion, encouraged her to pray and suggested she obtain holy water from San Damiano, Italy. San Damiano is a Marian shrine and site of alleged apparitions of the Blessed Virgin Mary. Anneliese told Monika she enjoyed visiting San Damiano and wished she could spend more time there. Because this shrine was important to Anneliese, there is a more detailed explanation in the Appendix. An Official Notification dated May 1, 1980 from the Bishop of Piacenza, Enrico Manfredini, expressed in summary a negative judgement on the alleged apparitions and messages of San Damiano, and stated that they had no supernatural foundation.

On June 3, 1970, while still in the hospital in Mittelberg, it struck a third time. There was stiffness in her arms, shortness of breath, and warm urine. Anneliese changed, moved to a clean bed and fell asleep.

On June 16, Anneliese went to Kempten to visit the neurologist Dr. Wolfgang von Haller. An EEG showed no disturbance of the brain; the same results Dr. Luthy had received. In spite of this, he prescribed an anti-convulsant drug.

Anneliese remained in the clinic for six weeks following her visit to Dr. Haller. On August 11, 1970, Dr. Haller checked Anneliese's EEG again and found no irregularities. On August 29, the long awaited day arrived. She was allowed to go home. Anneliese's sisters immediately noticed a change in her. She was moody. Roswitha complained about her behavior and queried as to what was wrong.

Chapter III

DEMONIC FACES and HORRID STENCHES

It is not exactly clear when the visions began, but during Anneliese's stay in Mittelberg, she began to see what she described to Dr. Luthy in September 1973 as Fratzen: ghastly demonic faces. She told him she saw these faces often, that the devil was in her and she felt empty inside. She further stated that a judgment of fire would be visited on everyone. In the fall of 1973 Anneliese relayed to Dr. Lenner that she experienced terrible stenches that she likened to burning fecal matter. At that point in time, only Anneliese smelled these stenches. The horrifying faces which reappeared several times before her release from Mittelberg left her depressed and frightened. She couldn't get these images and thoughts out of her mind.

Anneliese felt anxious going back to school to begin grade eleven as she was two years behind because of losing a year due to tuberculosis and pneumonia. Her schoolmate Ursula Kuzay described Anneliese as a shy, very religious person who put into practice what she believed. She also stated that Anneliese never spoke about her stay in the hospital in Mittelberg. Marie Burdich later told a court investigator: "After her illness, Anneliese was changed. She was quiet and withdrew from her friends. I also noticed that she wanted to carry on mostly religious conversations." [3]

Feeling alone and unwell, Anneliese's grades suffered. Following instructions from the sanatorium physicians, Anna took Anneliese to a specialist for lung diseases in Miltenberg in October, 1970. Dr. Reichelt asked Anna about the seizures noted in her daughter's file. Her lungs were fine but he noted circulatory problems and wrote a referral to Dr. Packhauser. Anneliese complained, as she and Anna were tired of running back and forth to doctor offices. Dr. Packhauser wrote to Dr. Vogt concerning her seizures and suggested a visit to a neurologist.

Dr. Vogt did not think a visit to a neurologist was necessary at that time. He did however prescribe an anti-convulsant. There is no evidence Anneliese took it for long. She was plagued by absences (brief occurrences of unconsciousness) and her body often became stiff. She struggled with depression and found it difficult to concentrate on her studies.

In late June 1972, Anneliese suffered another seizure-like attack. She was exhausted and apathetic. As September approached, they visited Dr. Luthy. Again, there were no irregularities with the EEG. In spite of this, he prescribed the anti-convulsant drug Zentropil (Dilantin). Dilantin is used primarily to treat grand mal epilepsy and psychomotor seizures. It has various potential side effects. It may affect the central nervous system or cardiovascular system. It may cause headaches, insomnia, skin rashes and affect the gums and liver. There is also evidence that Dilantin may cause birth defects. In October, the absences and body stiffness became more frequent. Anneliese returned for the prescribed checkups on January 18, March 27, and June 4 and 6, 1973 to monitor any side effects. Because no further seizures took place, Dr. Luthy believed the seizures were being suppressed. The EEG taken on June 4, 1973 was normal. In spite of this, the absences, demonic faces and horrid stenches continued.

In the spring of 1973, Anneliese began hearing knocking sounds in her room. Her mother didn't believe her. Anneliese was adamant. A visit to Dr. Vogt and an ear specialist confirmed no hearing problems. Her sisters heard the same sounds. There were rapping sounds from inside the closet, under the floor, and above the ceiling.

Anneliese talked to her parents about the demonic faces which were becoming more frequent. She also told them she heard voices stating she was damned to hell forever. Josef tried to convince Anna that Anneliese was epileptic and she would someday be well again. Anna related to Josef that she had witnessed Anneliese standing before their statue of the Blessed Virgin Mary with her face full of hatred and her eyes jet black.

In April, Anneliese was diagnosed with German measles. As a result, Anneliese visited their new family doctor, Dr. Kehler. In spite of missing several weeks of school, she passed the difficult Abitur exams and graduated. It was a time for celebration. Anneliese was in no mood or condition to celebrate.

In a conversation recorded by Father Renz on February 1, 1976 Anneliese described her state of mind at this time. [4]

> "It was especially gruesome at the time of the Abitur. Oh, Herr Pater, you cannot imagine that most awful dread (Grausen). It is a terror which goes through all my limbs and settles there. It is a dread that makes you think that you are right there, in the middle of hell. You are totally, utterly deserted. You can call all you want for help, to the Mother of God maybe, but they are all deaf. I think that is how it must have been for our Savior on the Mount of Olives, where they say he was beset by the shudders of death. Although I think for him it must have been worse, for, after all he had taken all the sins of the people on himself, all the sins of the world."

In the fall of 1973, Anneliese described to Dr. Lenner how she felt during this period. "In the last two years at the Gymnasium (1971-1973), I just didn't care beans about anything anymore. Things got worse and worse that way. I became completely apathetic in those years, with no interest in anything that was going on. I was able to perceive but not to experience. I felt like I was in a deep hole." She also told Dr. Lenner that she had recurring thoughts of suicide. [5]

Josef had enjoyed a pilgrimage to San Damiano arranged by Mrs. Thea Hein. He told Thea that one of his daughters was not well and they didn't know what was wrong with her. Josef thought a trip to San Damiano might be good for Anneliese.

When they arrived in San Damiano, Anneliese was unable to enter the shrine. She said that the soil burned like fire underfoot. She tried to enter from the back of the shrine but couldn't get past the garden. She also stated that she couldn't look at holy pictures or sacramentals. Thea offered Anneliese water from the miraculous well several times but she was unable to drink as she said it smelled bad. Josef bought her a medal but she couldn't wear it because she claimed it pressed her chest to the point that she could not breathe. Thea was wearing a medal around her neck under her dress. Anneliese tore it off by grabbing the outside of her dress. When leaving, Anneliese knocked Thea down on the bus and in doing so, broke her rosary. On the way home, Anneliese was still not herself. She seemed to be making fun of Thea and was using improper language. She spoke in a deep voice like a man. She exuded a stench, like fecal matter or something burning. Everyone on the bus could smell it. It was totally out of character for Anneliese to act in this manner. Josef sat beside her and held her tightly as he tried to calm her down. Thea suggested they include Anneliese in their prayer intentions. In spite of these occurrences, Anneliese and Thea became friends. Anneliese believed Thea could help her. She could discuss things with Thea she couldn't discuss with her mother. For example, there were times Anneliese did not take her medication. Thea stated that she would often pray for Anneliese. Anneliese told Thea that she knew the exact time and place Thea was praying for her. Thereafter Thea noted these occasions and confirmed what Anneliese told her. She told Thea Jesus related to her that there would come a time when the whole world would talk about hell and the devil. Anneliese didn't know what to make of this. Thea suggested that if she had the chance, to ask about this. Perhaps she misunderstood. Anneliese later told Thea that Jesus meant exactly what He said. Thea believes this prediction was fulfilled by the media attention brought to this story and the recent movies and renewed interest in her life. Thea also stated that Anneliese was visited by Jesus and Mary on many occasions. [6]

As the new school year approached, Anna pressured Anneliese to get ready for university. Anneliese told her mother she was in no condition to begin studying. She was feeling depressed and still seeing demonic faces.

Anna made an appointment to see Dr. Luthy on September 3, 1973. Anna later claimed in a police statement that Dr. Luthy had suggested consulting a Jesuit. Dr. Luthy vehemently denied under oath at the trial having said this. He stated he never used the term demonic possession and never said medical help would be of no benefit to Anneliese. He was never accused of the last two things that he denied. Anneliese never went back to Dr. Luthy. She visited specialists in Wurzburg and never again mentioned demonic faces or a judgment to visit the world.

Chapter IV

PRIESTS

The medication prescribed by Dr. Luthy made Anneliese depressed and tired. She suggested to her mother that maybe they should contact a priest, since the medication didn't seem to help. Thea suggested Father Habiger. The Michels wrote several letters to Father Habiger. Josef, Anna and Anneliese subsequently met with him to seek his advice. An associate priest of Father Habiger, Father Roth, sat in on the meeting. The Michels suspected Anneliese might be possessed. They discussed the trip to San Damiano. From their first meeting, Father Habiger found Anneliese entirely normal, somewhat shy, with no indications of possession. He suggested she see a specialist.

Having heard from the Michels that Dr. Luthy suggested consulting a Jesuit, Thea contacted Father Adolf Rodewyk in Frankfurt. Father Rodewyk was an expert in matters of possession, with several published books on the topic.

P. Adolf Rodewyk was born in 1894 in Koln Mullheim. He was a second lieutenant in the First World War. In 1918, he joined the Society of Jesus in the Netherlands. After studying theology in Bonn, Innsbruck and Valkenburg, he was ordained a priest in 1925. He later became rector of the college in Bad Godesberg and Hamburg and Superior in Koblenz and Bonn. During the Second World War, Father Rodewyk was Chaplain of the military hospital and also Novice master and rector of the Barmherzigen of brothers in Trier. It was in Trier where Father Rodewyk met a nurse who he ministered in a case of possession which was to become the well-known Magda case. In 1954, he became rector of the Ansgar School in Hamburg and Superior in Frankfurt in 1960. In Frankfurt he carried out his pastoral duties and taught Hebrew and Latin. In 1987, he moved into the retirement home for Jesuits in Munster where he resided until his death on November 9, 1989.

Based on what Thea told Father Rodewyk about Anneliese's trip to San Damiano, he requested a written account of the events. He responded by stating that he did see some indications of possession, but due to his advanced age (79) he was unable to become involved. He suggested contacting Father Herrmann in Aschaffenburg.

Anneliese saw Father Herrmann about ten times from the fall of 1973 to the summer of 1975. Father Herrmann found Anneliese to be a nice young lady, who was obviously from a deeply religious home. Anneliese complained about not having her own ego anymore. She attempted to, but was unable to describe the demonic faces in detail. He suggested that she see a neurologist. Anneliese told him that she had seen Dr. Luthy and he was unable to help her. Her parents told him of the disrespect Anneliese had at times for holy objects and that there were times when the stench of feces or something burning was in the room where she had been. Father Herrmann didn't experience these things during their meetings. They frequently prayed the rosary together. During these times, she was calm, pious, and showed no behavior that would lead him to suspect anything.

Father Roth was a friend of Father Ernst Alt. Father Roth mentioned that a member of a prayer group from his parish told him a young girl who traveled with them to San Damiano was said to be possessed. On several occasions they discussed Anneliese's case.

Father Alt was born in Eppelborn, Germany in 1937. He studied for the priesthood in Germany and Holland as a Montfort Father. His first posting was as chaplain to a hospital in Bonn where he worked with youth. Due to problems within the Montfort Fathers at the time, Father Alt was looking for a place where he could live his life as a priest the way he felt it should be lived. Father Alt eventually came under the Diocese of Wurzburg and was posted to St. Agatha's Parish in Aschaffenburg in 1971. [7]

Father Ernst Alt

The following is an excerpt from the defense's neurologist Dr. Lungershausen and psychiatrist Dr. Kohler's lengthy evaluation of Father Alt presented at the trial in 1978:

"He is polite in interpersonal contact, with very polished manners, occasionally pensive. His statements are carefully formulated, impressive, and convincing. He is fluent, very analytical, [and] has a large vocabulary demonstrating his schooling and extensive reading. His formal thinking processes are entirely undisturbed, even under prolonged questioning.

His visions which he describes, [see letter page 23] in their scenic and pictorial character, are not what might be expected, for instance, in the case of a schizophrenic psychosis. They must be considered rather as pseudo hallucinations.

In the case of Father Alt, we are dealing with an abnormal personality in the widest sense of the term. Parts of his prehistory, as he reported them, even suggest the presence of a psychosis of the schizophrenic type, although the findings cannot be construed as to pointing to any symptoms that could prove this diagnosis." [8]

The following is an excerpt of a letter from Father Alt to Bishop Stangl dated September 30, 1974 which sheds some light on why the doctors came to their conclusions about Father Alt: [9]

Ettleben, September 30, 1974

Most Reverend Bishop:

After much consideration and considerable hesitation, I should now like to acquaint you with a case of spiritual counseling about which I spoke to you very briefly when you were here for a visit.

This is the case of Anneliese Michel of Klingenberg. I will attempt to relate the case to you in order, as it happened.

My friend, Father Roth, came to me one evening and asked me to help him and some of his priest colleagues in solving a case of spiritual counseling. This concerned a girl, Anneliese Michel, whom he had not yet met. According to the opinion of some persons, she was alleged to be possessed or at least molested by the devil. I was supposed to tell, by tuning in on whatever she was radiating, whether she was sick or not.

Suddenly I was able to describe the whole family, father, mother, sisters, and grandmother, something I could not possibly know since I had never seen them. Later all of this could be verified. As to Anneliese, I felt an enormous radiation that originated from her neck or, rather, from her thyroid and her head. I did not detect any illness. This, of course, did not permit any conclusions as to whether she was possessed or not.

Two days later a fellow priest (Father Herrmann) who was going to take charge of the case visited me. He handed me two letters, one written by Anna Michel, the other by Anneliese. I was unable to read them because, all of a sudden, I became so nauseated that I thought that at any moment I was going to faint. I experienced a strange excitation such as I had never been subject to before, considerably frightening and startling my fellow priest, who was a witness to all of this. Naturally, even this experience, of course, did not prove we were dealing with a case of possession.

That evening I celebrated mass. I was mentally prepared for the transubstantiation (the moment in the mass when the transformation of the bread and wine into the body and blood of Christ occurs) and also included that unknown girl in the sacrifice. All of a sudden something hit me in the back, the air turned cold and, at the same time, there was an intense stench as though something was burning. I had to lean against the altar. With great effort and only a dint of considerable concentration was I able to speak the rest of the text. I felt deeply distressed, as if a negative force were surrounding me, which, however, aside from vexing me, could inflict no real harm.

After the service I went to a fellow priest and reported everything to him calmly and in detail.

The subsequent night was the most restless I have ever spent. I had taken a very effective sleeping pill, one that previously had always helped, but I could find no rest. My apartment was filled with a variety of stenches, as though something were burning of dung, of an open sewer, of fecal matter and these kept alternating. It didn't matter whether I reached out to the rosary or whether I spoke some other prayer, the stench continued. It was literally infernal. In addition, there was an occasional loud thumping in my wardrobe. I lay in bed, feeling sorely pressed. I tried to pray. In my own words I spoke an exorcism, thinking of my priestly power. For a few minutes I felt easier, but I was simultaneously ice cold and yet bathed in perspiration. In my extremity, I called to Father Pio for help, since I knew he had experienced similar tribulations. Nothing happened. I repeated my prayer to him and suddenly my room was filled with such an intense fragrance of violets that I thought I had dumped aftershave lotion on my pajamas. But it smelled only of my own sweat. Strangely, at the same time I stopped perspiring and my body felt warm. I breathed with relief and then only to discover, to my amazement, that my field of vision had been very much narrowed, and that my color perception was reduced. Now I was able to see colors once more in their normal intensity. The pressure on my head had disappeared. Before having to get up, I fell into an hour's restful sleep. "My night" had lasted from eleven the previous evening until five o'clock in the morning.

When, the following evening I told my fellow priests about all of this, they were suddenly able to smell the same strange stench. The entire parish house smelled as though of burning, although the windows were open.

The "molestations" did return a few more times, but they became less vivid, and if I prayed the exorcism prayer to myself, they stopped quite abruptly. Occasionally it was as if I had to struggle against them.

In the evening I took a walk with my friend, Father Roth, and once more as we talked about Anneliese Michel, we smelled the same series of stenches. Finally, now, I heard some of the details about the girl's affliction. [He listed them here.] A few weeks later I also met her personally. She was very depressed, but in our conversation she was able to express herself very clearly, and she obviously had a considerable gift of analysis.

In addition to the foregoing, during the trial Father Alt described two visions he experienced. The first occurred around Christmas 1975. Jesus was on the cross in anguish, and he heard a voice calling out: "for you." The second occurred two months later. He saw a woman with a small child surrounded with a brilliant light and once more a voice said: "for you". These were the "pseudo hallucinations" that Drs. Lungershausen and Kohler evaluated.

Several weeks later, Father Alt met Anneliese for the first time. She was pale and serious. She was looking for someone to believe her. Father Roth and Father Alt cross-examined her and concluded there was a possibility of possession. Father Alt sympathized with Anneliese, as he himself had experienced a few of the same things she had experienced. Although Anneliese's condition continued, she felt Father Alt was able to help her. Father Alt described Anneliese as mature, good natured and intelligent. She was very friendly and feminine in her demeanor. Anneliese was very direct, religious, and often helped her sisters resolve conflicts when they arose between them and their parents. She was honest and knew who she could trust. [10]

During a conversation with Father Alt, Anneliese's face suddenly changed, her eyes darkened in a way that the color of her eyes were no longer distinguishable, and she became absent. She said she was being molested. After he gave her his priestly blessing, she was normal again.

Anneliese was feeling better in the fall of 1973. In October, she registered at the Padagogische Hochscule in Wurzburg and began her studies, majoring in education and theology. After settling in at the Ferdinandeum (Catholic hostel) in Wurzburg, Anneliese became acquainted with many of the churches in her search for places to pray.

Anneliese missed her family. There were a few girls she knew from the Gymnasium in Aschaffenburg. Ursula Kuzay was her roommate and she also knew Karin Gora and Marie Burdich. Even though she took her medication regularly, and Father Alt visited her almost every two weeks, she felt depressed. The demonic faces continued to haunt her. Attending lectures was a struggle.

Father Alt often asked Anneliese the results or diagnosis of the physicians she visited. She once related to Father Alt that her condition was similar to epilepsy but not epilepsy.

In November, she went with her friends to a dance where she met Peter. Peter found Anneliese friendly, intelligent, animated, and fun to talk to. They saw each other often and attended several of the same courses together. Anneliese's friends saw an immediate difference in her. She was acting like a typical young lady in love.

Anneliese and Peter H

Two weeks after they met, Anneliese told Peter she couldn't see him anymore. She told him there were times when she was very depressed and her body became stiff. She said she couldn't feel what he felt for her. It was hard for her to explain. Peter was persistent. He suggested that there must be something a doctor could do for her. She was very interested in religion, whereas Peter hadn't been to church for several years. They continued to discuss her problem.

On November 27, 1973, Peter took Anneliese to see Dr. Lenner where she clearly outlined her condition. She was depressed, had no willpower, and couldn't listen or concentrate. She indicated that she liked Peter but it would not be right to continue to see him as she was unable to feel for him as she should.

Dr. Lenner asked her a lot of questions about her relationship with her parents. He felt she suffered from a case of neurosis caused by a domineering father and a mother whom she hated because she wasn't allowed to have any boyfriends. Based on Anneliese's description of her symptoms, Dr. Lenner suspected epilepsy as the cause of the seizures. He referred her to the University Neurological clinic.

The next day Anneliese went for an EEG. Dr. Irgmand Schleip, the academic director of the clinic, reported irregular patterns in the left temporal area of her brain. The previous five EEG's showed no abnormalities. She assumed it was epilepsy. Dr. Schleip switched her from Dilantin to Tegretol, since Dilantin hadn't completely suppressed the epilepsy-like activity in her brain. Tegretol, like Dilantin, has various potential side effects. It can cause fatigue, nausea and dizziness. Tegretol should only be prescribed after appraisal of patients with cardiac problems. As Tegretol affects the blood, suggested blood testing guidelines are: weekly for the first month, monthly for the first five months, and two to four times a year thereafter. There is no evidence that any blood tests were taken after her switch from Dilantin to Tegretol. Anneliese told Dr. Schleip of her homesickness for her family, and that she couldn't feel for Peter the way she felt she should. She also spoke of the nauseating stenches which Dr. Schleip thought were psychomotor seizures. Dr. Lenner diagnosed her ailments as psychological, and Dr. Schleip diagnosed them as physiological. She didn't mention the demonic faces to either of the doctors.

Peter tolerated Anneliese's depressed moods, which came and went unpredictably. They discussed religious matters and Peter started going to church again. It was only in December 1973 that Anneliese told Peter of the demonic faces and the stenches.

Anneliese told Peter that perhaps the switch to Tegretol had helped. However, it didn't help the horrid stenches which came without any visible source. Her whole family could smell them. Her depression coincided with the stenches and demonic faces. Peter suggested she might be hallucinating. Anneliese explained that when these things happened she had no control over herself and she had no say about anything. She struggled against this loss of control, but always lost. Peter suggested letting her make all the decisions.

In March 1974, Anneliese visited Father Alt. Although she was feeling better, things were bad again. The demonic faces remained in spite of her taking her medication regularly. At times she was unable to pray. She quickly improved when Father Alt prayed with and over her. Anneliese tried to visit Father Alt often as she felt his prayers and blessings helped. He thought she might be improving and suggested she practice a stricter religious lifestyle and continue her visits to the doctor. She saw Dr. Schleip in April 1974.

When Anneliese visited Dr. Lenner on May 7, 1974, she had been having severe headaches for some time, mainly in her forehead. This may have been a side effect of the Tegretol. Her reflexes were slow and she slept more than usual. As a result of her one side having paralysis like symptoms, Dr. Lenner referred her to Dr. Schleip. She suggested that perhaps Anneliese was not taking her medication on a regular basis. Dr. Schleip found her EEG improved, but wanted her to continue with Tegretol.

Anneliese's summer vacation was shortened due to her practice teaching. She visited San Damiano and Father Alt when suffering became too much to bear. Father Alt was caught between a natural explanation for Anneliese's problems and a supernatural one. He often discussed Anneliese's condition and possible causes with his priest friends in Aschaffenburg. They thought she was being molested by evil forces. To diagnose possession, several strict conditions had to be met. The demon had to control the body, rendering the person helpless. This didn't seem to be the case. In spite of this, Father Alt believed Anneliese was experiencing many things that could not be explained by epilepsy.

Father Alt had become Anneliese's spiritual director. A letter from Anneliese to Father Alt dated September 9, 1974 revealed her state at that time. [11]

Greetings, Father Alt:

I should like to write to you, although it is a difficult undertaking for me, because it is so hard for me to gather up my thoughts. Usually I can't commit to paper what I really want, and so I remain stuck in superficial matters.

Soon I will have to do my three week practice teaching. To be honest, I am terrified and am truly scared. Once more I realize I cannot cope with reality, which could be different, if yes, if I were master over myself. I am simply not in control and this often depresses me deeply. I can feel it especially when I am with other people or if I play the piano. In that case, I am especially aware of it or if I paint or write a letter. In fact, it doesn't really matter what I do, I simply feel it all the time. For this reason, I am never really satisfied when I work, or even afterwards. After all, a person normally puts his all into his work, he feels happy when he works, and he commits himself to it. I cannot understand why this is not the case with me. Why is it, that God denies me this happiness? Is it even possible for a human being to live without this dedication to his work or task without being fed up with himself without feeling superfluous and empty inside? I am asking myself this question over and over. It intrudes into my mind a thousand times a day. Why?

I admit things have become somewhat better. Life has taken on more meaning. Still, I am not alright yet. For instance, the following experience was a real shock for me. I wanted to do three weeks' vacation work in the hospital. I was there one day and got back home more in a trance than in ordinary consciousness. First of all, I was totally exhausted physically as early as 1:30 in the afternoon, but also psychologically. I was aggressive and somehow felt as though I had no relationship to the world around me. My parents, of course noticed what went on, and we took care of matters in such a way that Roswitha, my youngest sister, went to do the work. She finds it strenuous, too, but she seems to enjoy it nonetheless.

Last Saturday I went to confession. You know, one needs to overcome some resistance when one goes to confession, but as for me, that goes to the extreme. I often have the feeling as if all good spirits were deserting me on such occasions. Afterwards I was quite happy. On Sunday I received communion. I can feel there is a strength coming from that, although at the outset, I always feel completely empty, can sense nothing, and have the feeling that I cannot relate to anything. But this empty feeling disappears after a few minutes. I become more myself and feel well.

Just imagine, the last time Bishop Stangl visited here, he asked for lay people to help give out Holy Communion. It is my opinion that even hand communion is not proper, but to let lay persons hand it out— that is really shocking. As for me, I will never accept communion from a lay person. After all, we are not in a situation of crisis. The hands of a lay person are not consecrated; they should not touch the Holy Eucharist.

Peter no longer wants to come to our house because he cannot be alone with me and because Mama behaves in such an impossible way. For instance, she won't allow him to come to my room with me. It's ridiculous. She also made the rule he should come to see me only once a week. Perhaps you could talk with her sometime.

At night I often cried to myself... There was no one to whom I could have gone and talked. Then I did not cry anymore, because it was no use. After a while I could not even cry. Then I became very ill –pleurisy and TB– and I felt even lonelier and more helpless than ever. My mother had so much work, I told her nothing, and things got progressively worse. I felt that God had deserted me entirely. I was considerably molested at that time already. I always wanted to kill myself. I was deathly afraid I might become insane because I was so desperate. Then I felt God had not deserted me completely. I was able to pray again. I felt better and recovered. But, unfortunately, I then had to go to the sanatorium in Mittelberg (1970). There things went downhill, I suffered torture there. Prayer did not help me, and there was nothing else either. Then there was something like a recovery when I was released after a half a year, but somehow I was dead inside. At least now you may be able to empathize a little better with me. I think I will come to see you soon.

Until then,
Anneliese

On September 17, 1974, Anneliese called Father Alt. She was very depressed. Her state of depression had become constant. After praying with her and giving her his blessing, she felt better. In a letter dated September 9, 1974 to Bishop Stangl, Father Alt described Anneliese's condition. Father Alt asked the Bishop's permission for the solemn exorcism to be used in times of crisis. He suggested it be done in secret as to maintain its sacredness and avoid any religious sensation. Father Alt's request was denied and he was counseled to be patient and continue as he had been doing.

Perhaps due to Anneliese's increased religious lifestyle, she saw less of some of her former friends and made a few new ones. Anna Lippert, Maria Klug and Anneliese formed a prayer group. They exchanged religious literature and discussed the changes taking place in the Church in Germany. They didn't support the change of the mass being said in German and didn't believe in receiving communion in the hand. As a result, they attended mass where these changes hadn't been implemented.

Some of the girls on the same floor at the PH dormitory considered these girls to be a bit different. They could be heard praying the rosary in their room. There were holy pictures on the wall and a holy water font at the door.

In January 1975, Anneliese went to see Dr. Schleip. The EEG showed nothing new and she was to continue taking Tegretol. Anneliese lost her appetite, looked very pale, and was depressed. At times she stayed in bed for several days.

On May 15, 1975, Anneliese's grandmother Oma Furg died. Barbara was working away from home and Gertraud was in Fatima, Portugal for the summer. Only Roswitha was home when Anneliese came to visit on weekends. As Anneliese's condition had worsened, Father Alt suggested a checkup. Dr. Kehler was satisfied with her condition but referred her back to Dr. Schleip. On June 13, 1975, Dr. Schleip told Anneliese her EEG was encouraging but there were still concerns and she must continue taking Tegretol. She also told Anneliese that while taking Tegretol marriage wasn't an option due to the potential side effects, and the medication would likely only be required for another six months.

Chapter V

ANNELIESE OUT OF CONTROL

Anneliese added music to her majors of education and theology. She chose to write her thesis on "Overcoming Anxiety as a Task of Religious Education." The heavy workload, combined with her condition, caused her to contemplate dropping out of university. Later, she related to Peter how she felt at this time. Inside, she kept hearing a voice telling her she was eternally damned. It was a struggle to convince herself there was no reason why she would be damned.

On June 28, 1975, Anneliese, Roswitha and Peter visited Father Alt. Anneliese related that she could no longer control herself. She wanted Peter and the girls around but would suddenly and uncontrollably throw things at them. She pleaded for help. After the usual prayers and blessing, she improved, but not for long.

On the following Tuesday, Father Alt visited Anneliese in Wurzburg. He found her in deep despair. She repeated that she was condemned. Shortly after they began to pray a rosary, she was unable to continue. Tears ran down her face. She acknowledged she had been taking her medication. At the end of their meeting, Father Alt prayed the exorcismus probativus to himself. She immediately stood as if to defend herself and ripped the rosary to pieces. When Peter arrived, she told him, in a deep guttural voice, to leave. Father Alt was now convinced of Anneliese's possession. His prayers, unlike before, were providing little or no relief.

As Father Alt was leaving, he noticed a discarded piece of paper containing notes in Anneliese's handwriting. Upon further examination, he realized the depth of Anneliese's desperation and her heart wrenching cry for help.[12]

> courage leaves, to say what I wanted.
> I am a sinner; I have clearly recognized that in the chapel today, even if I imagined something different. I ... I am
> I have no courage, despaired.
> I am afraid that my priest... my
> no trust

> I am standing at the crossroads, either… life or death…Grievously injured… through the years, I no longer defended myself … not now either… I became desperate after Holy Communion, in spirit and heart. An iron chain is pressing around my heart. Fear, terror… my spirit is lame, if it becomes free, freer… right away despair rises the worst of it is that I have no choice anymore, I see
> that sometimes clear like lightning, hopelessness sits
> at the root where life is
> it has become a condition
> pride, unspeakable pride will not set me free
> when I speak, my heart does not speak along
> I am afraid that people despair in me
> paralysis
> still I give myself every glimmer of hope… newly up…fettered
> … things will get worse and worse for me day after day if no dam will be constructed.

Father Alt was deeply concerned. He called the Michels and suggested they come and take Anneliese home. On July 17, they came to pick her up. The following day, they visited Dr. Schleip, desperately trying to find out the cause of her condition and the prospects of overcoming it. Dr. Schlep explained there was indication of an epileptic focus in the left temporal lobe leaving them no more hopeful than before.

Anneliese's friends recalled several events at this time. Once, Maria Klug and Anna Lippert were talking with Anneliese when suddenly she told them to stop praying, that it hurt, even though neither had been praying out loud. Another time Anneliese removed a picture of Jesus from her wall. More importantly, she no longer went to mass. She complained she couldn't get past the entrance of the church. At times she couldn't bend her legs.

Anna Lippert recalled the following:

> "I remember an incident from July 1975. I sat with her in her room, and her boyfriend Peter, was also present. Suddenly, right in the middle of the conversation, her face contracted into a real Fratze, a hideous, grimacing countenance I cannot describe in detail. Her body became completely stiff. It took half an hour before the cramp disappeared. Her boyfriend explained to me that her condition was due to the fact she was possessed. I too thought it must be a possession, for her grimace was so demonic I could think of nothing else." [13]

Back home, Anneliese began to eat. Her legs were stiff like stilts and she had trouble getting around the house. She dragged herself along holding on to tables, chairs and whatever she could put her hands on. It was clear that she was constantly frightened by something and she couldn't sleep. She could no longer do the only thing that gave her relief, which was to pray. Thea Hein suggested asking Father Roth for help, since Father Alt was so far away. Father Roth decided to come and see for himself. Father Roth recounted the visit in a statement to police:

> Herr Michel received me and took me immediately to the living room. It was filled with a horrible stench, of something burning, and of dung, that penetrated

everything. Herr Michel expressly called my attention to it and told me Anneliese had been in the room just before. In other rooms of the Michel home and on the outside, I could detect no trace of the stench.

I went to the kitchen with Herr Michel and there Fraulein Michel came running toward me, as if she wanted to assault me. About one meter away from me she suddenly stopped, very stiffly, without saying anything at all. After a few seconds she ran away again and then ran towards me once more stopping a short distance in front of me in a rigid posture.

I should like to say here parenthetically that Herr Michel told me during this visit that after he had talked to me on the phone, she had said, "Roth that dog, he is also going to come," although he told her nothing of my intended visit.

After running towards me twice and then standing still in this manner, Anneliese began raging and screaming very loudly. "Get out", she shouted at me, "You are tormenting me". Her parents asked me to stay, so I remained in the kitchen. Thereupon Anneliese tore up a rosary and threw the pieces on the floor.

Herr Michel took me outside and told me other details that took place while his daughter was having these attacks of rage. Both the family and Frau Hein then entreated me to say a blessing over Anneliese. But when I attempted to take my crucifix out of my breast pocket which she did not know I carried with me— the demon in the girl began to rage.

It finally went so far that she attempted to throw a five liter container of water from San Damiano at me. Interestingly, the jug fell from her raised arms, landing beside her instead of hitting me. [14]

It had been over a week since Anneliese was out of the house. She couldn't walk normally as she was not able to bend her legs. She also had trouble speaking. It was a particularly trying time for Anna due to Anneliese's condition and behavior. One Sunday afternoon in July 1975, Anna asked Peter if he would take Anneliese for a drive. After Anna helped Peter settle Anneliese in the car they drove to a quiet country road near Rollbach just east of Klingenberg. They pulled over, parked, and set out for a walk. It was excruciatingly slow. Suddenly Anneliese stopped and dropped to her knees. Peter motioned to Anneliese to stand up as he was concerned someone might see her kneeling. Peter tried to communicate with Anneliese several times but she was unresponsive and appeared to be in a trance. Approximately ten minutes later, Anneliese stood up and shouted with excitement, "I can walk, look at me! I'm free! I'm free!" Peter was amazed at the sudden change in Anneliese's physical and emotional condition. He asked her what had happened to bring about this sudden change. Anneliese replied that she had seen the Blessed Virgin Mary.

Unable to contain their excitement, Peter and Anneliese rushed home to share the good news with her sisters and her parents. Anneliese ran upstairs and exclaimed to her mother, "Mom, mom look at me! I can walk again, I can jump, I can dance! The Mother of God appeared to me!" After a brief silence, "Yes, yes the Mother of God appeared to me!" She repeated this several times. When Anna asked where Peter was, Anneliese explained that he was so overcome with emotion he remained in the car. Peter and Anneliese both gave an account to Anna of what had happened.

Approximately two months later, Anneliese had another apparition of the Blessed

Virgin Mary at Engelberg Monastery, a Franciscan monastery and overlooking the town of Grossheubach where Anneliese would o̶ Here the Mother of God lamented to Anneliese, "It is a great sufferi̶ that so many souls are lost! It is necessary to do penance for priests, for for your country. Would you like to do penance for these souls so that ̶ are lost?" [15] [16]

Anneliese immediately explained and discussed with Anna the request m̶ ̶ ̶o her by the Blessed Virgin Mary. She had three days to consider it: to accept it or to reject it. Anna in turn discussed it with Josef. They were very concerned. [17] [18]

Anneliese spent the next days kneeling and standing before a crucifix. When Anna suggested to Anneliese that she could not go through with this, Anneliese responded, "I can mom. If I don't, souls may be lost!" [19]

It appears Anneliese's affirmative response to the Blessed Virgin Mary was communicated a few days later in the kitchen in Anna's presence as Anna heard Anneliese say: "Mother Mary, you are so beautiful!" Anna wasn't able to understand anything else, as Anneliese seemed to be in a trance. [20]

Anneliese told her mother that for a couple of weeks after this vision she was totally free. Anneliese told Peter things would soon get bad again. Anneliese returned to Wurzburg in August to register for the fall semester. Upon returning to her room, she became completely rigid. She stood in front of the crucifix hanging on the wall with a gaze of hatred. Her face was distorted and she growled like an animal. Peter started to pray for her silently and she immediately ordered him to stop. Peter was sometimes afraid to be alone with Anneliese as he could not communicate with her. Fearing things could get worse Peter took her back to Klingenberg.

Meanwhile, Father Roth had reported his experience with Anneliese to Father Alt. They agreed that she was under the influence of demonic forces and perhaps these forces were now using her body, thus adding to the criteria needed to prove she was suffering from possession. With this new evidence, Father Alt felt it was time to address the issue once again with the Bishop. As Bishop Stangl was on vacation, Father Alt phoned him and obtained verbal permission to perform the small exorcism prayers. On August 3, 1975, Father Alt and Father Roth went to Klingenberg to begin their mission.

During the praying of the small exorcism, Anneliese whimpered and moaned that she was burning. She also tried to knock the book containing the exorcism prayers out of Father Alt's hand.

Father Alt decided to contact Father Rodewyk. As Father Alt was planning a holiday, he asked Father Rodewyk whether he should cancel his vacation or carry on as planned. On August 16, 1975, while on holidays, Father Alt wrote to the Bishop updating him on Anneliese's progress. There was little improvement and she seemed to be in a trance.

Meanwhile back at the Michel home, things had gone from bad to worse as Anneliese was in a frenzied state. She had only one to two hours of rest per night. Sometimes she would shout the prayer my Jesus forgiveness and mercy, forgiveness and mercy... for hours on end. She knelt down, got up, knelt down, and got up quickly and so often, that her knees swelled and were ulcerated. She ran through the house screaming, and after long periods, would tremble and twitch, then collapse and remain rigid for several days.

Sometimes the muscles in her neck would tense up like bands of steel. She couldn't eat any solid foods and could drink fluids only sparingly. This rigidity spread to her chest and she had to struggle to breathe. When Anna tried to put a pillow under her head to try and help her, Anneliese asked her not to help or she would be forced to undergo something worse. When Josef tried to hold her up, Anneliese turned red as she choked and gasped for air.

While she was not allowed to eat, she ate flies and spiders. She urinated on the kitchen floor. Everyone learned to duck to avoid being kicked, punched or bitten. She ripped holy pictures off the wall, tore rosaries apart, and shattered a crucifix on the corner of a bed. Sometimes during the heat of the day she would put her head in the toilet. Once she rolled around in the coal dust and then climbed into bed.

There were days when Anneliese fought with Peter and her sisters from morning until night. Peter's shirts were torn and the sleeves ripped off. By evening they were all exhausted. [21]

On the eve of the feast of the Assumption of the Blessed Virgin Mary Anneliese prayed through the night until the following morning. Later when she was herself again, she told Peter that August 15 was the worst day of her life. She was not able to pray or enter the church, as she felt prevented from entering by an invisible force. When the exorcism prayers were said quietly, it felt like her hands were in a wasps nest. For some time the demons had tempted Anneliese with despair and thoughts of suicide. She was tempted to jump out the window or into the river.

One day Anneliese was under the kitchen table barking like a dog. Everyone tried to get her to come out. Nothing worked. Josef thought to call Thea Hein who came and found her under the table. She instructed Anneliese three times in the name of the Blessed Trinity to come out and sit down. Like a lamb she slowly came out and took a seat at the table. [22]

Around this time, Anneliese told Peter that grandma Furg, who had died three months earlier, and Martha, her deceased sister, came to comfort her. Also, small but clearly visible oval wounds had opened on her feet. She insisted that these wounds were not self-inflicted. She continued to feel pain in her feet after the wounds had healed.

Anna related the following: "One morning I entered Anneliese's room and said, Anneliese, you are in bed today. I usually found her kneeling before the crucifix or doing some other form of penance. I noticed the wounds on her feet which were very swollen. This had occurred during the night. She later received the same on her hands. Her hands were not as bad as her feet. She suffered very much from these wounds." [23]

Peter, Roswitha and her parents took two hour shifts attempting to prevent Anneliese from injuring herself as the situation became unbearable. They tried to contact Father Alt who was on vacation. Thea contacted Father Rodewyk in Frankfurt. He decided not to interrupt Father Alt's vacation. Instead, Father Rodewyk decided to come to Klingenberg and observe Anneliese himself. In early September 1975, Father

Rodewyk traveled by train to Aschaffenburg. Thea and Father Herrmann picked him up and drove him to Klingenberg. In a subsequent statement, he described his visit to the Michel home:

> When I entered the house, Anneliese Michel lay, fully dressed, on the floor of the kitchen and could obviously not be addressed. I am of the opinion she was in a typical hypnotic state, in a kind of deep sleep.
> I should like to remark that such a state is a symptom of possession. I designated it as a crisis situation.
> First I went to the living room with her parents and had them report to me about the condition of their daughter. Then I directed them to bring Anneliese into the room and make her sit on the sofa.
> Her father led her in and held her by the hand because she tried to hit her parents. She did not look emaciated.
> I sat down beside her and held her hands. In her trance state, a second personage announced itself, calling itself Judas. I had asked, "What is your name?" and her answer came, "Judas." She spoke with an altered, much lower voice.
> I had held her by the wrists. During the conversation I noticed that her cramped muscles relaxed. She came to and looked at me with surprise. Apparently it was not until then that she noticed me consciously. Subsequently I was able to carry on an entirely reasonable conversation with her. I told her that we would not desert her and we would help her. I was thinking of priestly aid through exorcism...
> Suddenly the cramps started again. I asked her family to take her back to the kitchen. I told them I knew enough about the case, that I found confirmation of my surmise that we were dealing with a case of possession, and that I would have to consider what could be done. When I left the house, Anneliese came out of the kitchen and slapped my cheek. [24]

As Father Rodewyk left for the door, Anneliese was playing the piano as if nothing happened.

For Father Rodewyk, important elements in defining possession were now present. The spirit's name had been revealed and Anneliese showed an aversion to consecrated objects and a fear of exorcism.

Sometimes Anneliese wanted to eat, but wasn't allowed to. She either couldn't open her mouth or couldn't swallow. This condition would come and go, much to her parents concern. On at least one occasion, Anneliese could not swallow after receiving Holy Communion.

As soon as Father Alt returned from his vacation, Father Rodewyk called him to update him on Anneliese's condition. As far as he was concerned, this was definitely a case of possession. He suggested they get together to consult on how to proceed.

A few days later, Fathers Alt, Rodewyk, Roth and Habiger met in Aschaffenburg. Father Rodewyk read his opinion wherein he stated that in his view this was clearly a case of demonic possession. Initially, Italy was discussed as a location to perform the exorcism as exorcisms were common in certain churches there. This was rejected as it would be hard to protect Anneliese's privacy. To avoid any publicity, they agreed that Father Alt write the Bishop and ask for formal permission to perform an exorcism as in the Roman Ritual. Initially Father Alt's name was put forward to perform the exorcism. Father Roth thought Father Arnold Renz, superior of the Salvatorian monastery of Ruck-Schippach, might be a suitable candidate for the job. He was considered a pious priest and he lived close to Klingenberg.

Father Arnold Renz

Father Alt visited Father Renz to discuss the case and ask him if he would be interested in performing the exorcism. After considering the request for several days, Father Renz gave his consent.

In a letter written to Bishop Stangl, Father Alt discussed their previous conversations and attached a copy of his last written report on Anneliese's possible possession. He informed him that Father Rodewyk was now involved in the case and he had formed an Opinion, outlining the reasons why he believed possession was present in this case. The Bishop was informed that Father Renz had been contacted and agreed to take on this matter, subject to the Bishop's approval. Father Rodewyk counseled the whole issue be dealt with incognito, and suggested referring to Anneliese as Anna Lieser to protect her identity. Father Alt discussed the certainty and agreement among the priests that they were dealing with a case of possession, that Anneliese was suffering tremendously and immediate action was necessary. Father Alt's letter was hand delivered, accompanied by Father Rodewyk's Opinion.

Bishop Josef Stangl

Bishop Stangl responded with the following letter to Father Renz:

The Bishop of Wurzburg

September 16, 1975
To The Superior Father Arnold Renz
Strictly Confidential
8751 Elsenfeld-Ruck-Schippach

Reverend Fellow Priests,

After due consideration and with good information, I now charge the Reverend Father Renz, Salvatorian, Superior in Ruck-Schippach to proceed with Anna Lieser within the terms of CIC can 1151 1. For some time my prayers have been directed to this concern. May God give us his help. I thank everyone sincerely for their efforts.

With best wishes and my blessing,
+ Josef
Bishop of Wurzburg

Chapter VI
EXORCISM SESSIONS

Wilhelm "Arnold" Renz was born in 1911 in Hiltensweiler, near Lake Constance in southern Germany. He attended high school and University of the Salvatorian order in Lochau. He did his novitiate in Heinzendorf/Schlesien (Poland) and studied theology in Passau, Germany. He was ordained a priest in 1938. His first posting was as a missionary in Shaowu, in the Fukien province, China. He remained in China until he was expelled by the Communists in 1952. His first posting upon returning to Germany was as a pilgrimage priest in Maria Steinbach. He then worked as chaplain at St. Willibald's parish in Woffenbach. In 1965 he became superior of the monastery and pastor of St. Pius X parish, in Ruck-Schippach. The church was funded by an organization founded by the German mystic and Franciscan tertiary Barbara Weigand. Father Renz had studied her writings.

Father Renz was considered by his peers to be pious, intelligent and charitable. Anneliese trusted him as her spiritual advisor and saw him as a kind and gentle father figure.

Helge Cramer is a German film producer from Pottenstein, near Nuremberg. He has produced documentaries on the Klingenberg case and interviewed most of the people involved in the case. During the trial in 1978 he witnessed several days of the proceedings in Aschaffenburg. He shared the following on Fathers Renz and Alt:

> "Father Renz was a straight and honest man. He was kind and friendly. He was a trusting individual who perhaps was oblivious to those around him who might cause him harm. He loved nature and liked to take long walks and hike in the mountains. He spoke openly and frankly about the case. He totally believed in the possession of Anneliese.
>
> Father Alt was a serious man with a strong character. He believed that by the providence of God, he was a witness to the events in Klingenberg. He too was totally convinced of Anneliese's possession. He felt his role was to be in the background and defend the truth as he had witnessed it. He never sought attention for himself."

Father Renz was well aware that Father Rodewyk was an expert in the field of exorcism and had previously read his book *Exorcism Today*. While waiting for Bishop Stangl's authorization to proceed with the exorcism, he also read Father Rodewyk's *Exorcism According to the Roman Ritual*.

On September 23, 1975, the day Father Renz received the Bishop's letter, he visited the Michels. Father Renz found Anneliese exhibiting no signs of possession. To the contrary, he found her quite reserved, polite and deeply religious. He returned the next day to perform the first exorcism rite.

On arrival, Father Renz was accompanied upstairs by Anneliese's sisters Roswitha and Barbara, her parents, her boyfriend Peter, Peter Hein and Fathers Alt, Herrmann and Roth. An altar was set up on a side table covered by an embroidered tablecloth. On it stood a statue of Jesus and framed pictures of the Blessed Virgin Mary, the Sacred Heart of Jesus, St. Michael the archangel and Padre Pio. Chairs were set up around the perimeter of the room.

The first exorcism session, according to the Roman Ritual, began at about 4:00 pm September 24. Before the session began, Anneliese spoke and laughed with everyone. She then asked Father Alt to hold her hands because she did not know what was going to happen. After behaving quietly at the beginning of the exercise, Anneliese reacted violently to the sprinkling of holy water. When Father Renz made the sign of the cross over her or sprinkled her with holy water, Anneliese roared and raged and her body trembled and twitched. One could perceive the hatred in her facial expressions. She was fully aware of her actions and heard everything spoken through her by the demons, unlike some previous documented cases, where the victim was totally unaware of what was taking place. Later, when Father Alt asked Anneliese what she saw, she responded: "I only observed and had no influence on what was happening. I am only in the background, just looking on."

Josef, Peter and Peter Hein held Anneliese as she attempted to bite and kick those before her. In spite of being restrained by the three men, she continued to struggle. At times she screamed and howled like a dog. She often repeated: "Put away that shit" (holy water), or "stop with that shit." To all the required textbook questions, such as what is your name, reason for possession, when are you leaving etc., no answers were provided. Father Renz prayed again and again in the name of the Blessed Trinity and called upon the intercession of the Blessed Virgin Mary and the angels and saints to expel the demons from Anneliese. At the end, when the group prayed, Anneliese was furious. The first session lasted approximately 3.5 hours. All those present, especially Anneliese, placed all their hopes in the exorcisms to end the possession, so life could get back to normal.

Since Father Renz read in Latin, led the prayers, sprinkled holy water, made the sign of the cross or touched his stole to Anneliese's forehead for a blessing etc., all according to the ritual, there was no time for him to write an account of what was transpiring. From September 29 on, at the suggestion of Thea Hein, he began to tape record the sessions. Thea and Josef also recorded the sessions. Father Renz later produced two tapes which highlighted the more important sessions. Father Alt played this tape for Bishop Stangl during a visit with him in Wurzburg. Anneliese had expressed her approval that the tapes be given to the Bishop.

For those involved (the priests, Anneliese's parents and sisters, Peter, and the Hein's), all came to believe that Anneliese suffered molestations and a malevolent entity had taken over her will, not her soul. Often her words and deeds were not her own. Anneliese experienced everything that was going on as though she was spying from the hole she spoke of. She stated that the demons were using her voice, and she was a spectator who couldn't prevent what they were doing to her. Father Renz described how sometimes it was like someone was shaking Anneliese, and other times it was as though she was jerked as if she was pushed from behind.

The words of the demons which appear on the following pages were transcribed from the exorcism sessions. It is necessary to state that although these words are important to this story, it does not mean that what was said is true. Very often in exorcisms, the truth is intermingled with falsehood. These words are gathered without giving an opinion as to what is true and what is not true. For example, when they say the apparitions of San Damiano will be recognized by the Church in the future, this may or may not be true. Here, we simply present the facts without considering their credibility.

September 29, 1975:

Father Renz stated that Anneliese began to tremble when he arrived for this session.

Lucifer (several times): "The pretentious one is obsessed. This is our work. She cannot take any exams. I'll take care of it. The snotnose is cursed. I will not let her free. I will not get out alone. And we are so many inside her! The snotty slut is ours! You have to pray much more. By order of that one (Virgin Mary) they should still recite... (rosary) or else, we cannot come out. This affair will last at least for half a year still. By order of that Lady, people should fast. She was cursed from the beginning. She was cursed before birth!"

Judas: "People standing during Holy Communion. This pleases me more than kneeling, I hate it. That thing that you wear, (cassock) the great majority do not wear it any more. They no longer obey the Pope in Rome. It is the one in Rome who keeps the Church going. (To Father Renz) I know you have been to China and there you have offended me much. You snatched souls from me. The one from Frankfurt (Father Rodewyk) has expelled me several times, but now he can no longer do so as he is old. That other one (Gertraud), goes down there to Portugal (Fatima) and preaches of that one (the Virgin Mary) and speaks of the apparitions in 1917. No one believes in them now days. That one is taking so many from me, the snotty slut, that stupid, that cursed one."

During subsequent exorcism sessions, Father Renz tried to identify the demons by name. Typical responses included "arsehole, sow," etc. "Go on, babble all day, I'm not leaving. (…) No, no, she belongs to me, get out of here you carcass, no, she belongs to me, to me." Father Renz asked how it was that they disturbed Anneliese at her Abitur. "We got her all confused in German literature, in that hour that she was in there, she didn't know back from front. We had permission. She still passed." Anna shouts from the back: "Yes, because she, the Lady, she wanted that."

The demons remarked that people no longer believed in religious books, hell or the positive effects of prayer, especially the rosary. They hated sacred things, holy persons and places of pilgrimage. They argued and lied among themselves. At times they didn't seem to be very powerful since the Blessed Virgin Mary seemed to be able to control them if desired, and force them to reveal things against their wills. According to the voice that came from Anneliese's mouth, sometimes Barbara Weigand, Padre Pio or Theresa Neumann was present.

Barbara Weigand (1845-1943) was a peasant who received revelations from the Blessed Virgin Mary and St. Michael the archangel aimed at renewing religious life and the life of priests. To this end, she founded the Eucharistic League of Love. In 1886, she wrote down the revelations she received. At the time, these revelations were not taken seriously by the hierarchy of the Church. Barbara Weigand's cause for beatification began in 1975.

Anneliese felt an attraction to these writings from which she made notations for herself. Her interior life was greatly enriched by these writings.

Padre Pio (1887-1968) now St. Pio, was a stigmatized Capuchin priest who lived a remarkable mystical life. Padre Pio was frequently attacked by the devil, both physically and spiritually. On many occasions the devil appeared to him in his cell as an angel of light, a dog or in other forms.

Theresa Neumann (1898-1962) was a German mystic and stigmatic. She suffered the passion of Jesus most of her life. From 1922 until her death in 1962, Theresa consumed no food other than the Holy Eucharist. From 1926 until her death she drank no water. This phenomenon is commonly referred to as inedia. She was one of the most accessible mystics of this kind. Many experts, physicians and people from all walks of life came to visit her. Proceedings began for her beatification in 2005.

Among the evil ones, Judas was the first to own up to his name, then Lucifer, and later Nero, who stated: "I am the third of the covenant." The remaining named participants were Cain, Hitler and Fleischmann a fallen priest. After one of the exorcism sessions Anneliese asked Father Alt to explain to her what the demons had said.[25]

When speaking of exorcism, it is in reference to the exorcism of demons, although this expression is properly defined as including fallen angels and souls who have been condemned. It has been demonstrated over the centuries that when a priest exorcizes a possessed person, fallen angels or condemned souls have manifested themselves (speaking through the possessed person). Afterwards, the term is typically simplified by referring to the "expulsion of demons." When various persons are named (Nero, Hitler, Cain, etc.), it does not mean for certain that these persons are condemned. As stated, the words spoken are not always true. These words need to be compared with other information, if or where applicable. For example, in the case of Judas, the words of the demons may be confirmed by the words of the Gospel: "It was better for him, if that man had not been born" (Mark 14:21) or "and none of them were lost, but the son of perdition, that scripture may be fulfilled" (John 17:12). If one is saved, it is obvious that it is worth being born. Here the Gospel corroborates the logical conclusion that Judas was condemned. In the case of Nero, he appears in other cases of exorcism, allowing one to suspect that he also is condemned. There have been several personages (names of demons and people) who have repeatedly appeared in cases of possession over the centuries. When Nero speaks about his importance in the society of Hell, this may be completely false.

During one session, Anneliese grabbed Thea by the throat and it took two of the men to come to her rescue. Thea spoke of the incident: "She had the strength of a bear, yet she was a delicate thing. You can't imagine the strength she had. I thought at the time she would ring my neck. Five men were there, the priest, Peter my husband, Mr. Michel, Peter and I believe Father Alt. I thought she was going to strangle me." [26] Peter Hein demonstrated for me (the author of this book) by grabbing my arm to show how he used to hold Anneliese by putting his arm under hers and holding her to himself. I can attest to the fact that at seventy-five years of age, he still is a powerful man. [27]

On one occasion Father Renz brought in three unmarked glasses of water. One contained holy water from Lourdes, one water from San Damiano, the other tap water. When Anneliese picked up the water from San Damiano she commented: "San Damiano shit water." She only drank the tap water. [28] Many priests and laypersons believe that by drinking holy water it is possible to discern if someone is suffering possession. This is not true in all cases. There are cases where the possessed person can drink holy water without the demons showing signs of loathing. The holy water disgusts them, but sometimes they can resist and put up with it. In other cases, the pain and reactions of screaming, insults etc. are immediate.

Anneliese once stated: "I can speak any language but feel free to speak to me in German." Although Father Renz normally read from his prayer book in Latin, on one occasion he spoke freely without his book. Anneliese immediately pointed out that he had made a mistake and his Latin was poor. It was also astonishing to the priests to see Anneliese's immediate responses to questions put to her in Dutch and Chinese. [29]

Demons understand all languages because, in addition to having a higher intellect than human beings, they have existed since the creation of the world. Their knowledge of the dead languages has been proven in many cases of possession throughout history. However, there are some misconceptions regarding this. For the most part, demons do everything possible not to make themselves known. Although a priest will ask or order them to answer certain questions, they often remain silent. Even in cases where demons are outspoken, they tend to speak of trivialities. The demon who understands a question in a language unknown by the possessed person usually answers in the native language of the person possessed.

The different demons could be identified by the way they spoke, the tones of their voices and their expressions. Their character traits were revealed. When Lucifer spoke through Anneliese, he spoke in a majestic way, intelligently and always quick to the point. When Hitler spoke, he barked. Although the voices and expressions changed, the words were always in Anneliese's native Franconian dialect. When Anneliese spoke, she spoke loudly in an altered guttural voice, unlike her normal reserved self.

With regards to Fleischmann, the following is a summary from a taped conversation given by Father Alt to Dr. Goodman in July, 1979: [30]

> When I became pastor of the parish in Ettleben, the church was in bad condition and I had the task of having it restored. I made a search of the church documents to discover who had building authority for the church (Germany has no separation of church and State), the community or possibly the state. I went to the repository of the village, the files of which are complete since 1646 and contain scattered documents of even earlier centuries, clear back to the founding of the parish in 1288. As I was going through these papers, I came across a file of priests who had been pastors in Ettleben since about 1300. In glancing through it, my attention was caught by a notation on a Pastor Fleischmann. The name was totally unknown to me, and I started reading what this man may have been up to. He was characterized as concubinarius, that is, a womanizer. His daughter Martha's gravestone from the sixteenth century can still be seen in Ettleben; he was vin adicto, in other words a drunkard; he had four children, and was a brutal bully. One day he beat a man to death right in the parish house. There was also a report that he had battered a woman so fiercely that for weeks and months she remained in the care of the barber in Wurzburg.
>
> In the fall of 1975 I [Father Alt] went for a visit to Klingenberg. I had been in Ettleben over a year and a half by then, and I was asked, "Well and how are things in Ettleben, with the restored church and all that?" And I said, half in jest, "Let's see now, of course there have always been bad pastors in Ettleben, and perhaps I am also one of those; at any rate there was one who killed another man." This was during a pause in the exorcism. We sat there relaxing, drinking tea, when suddenly Anneliese began to scream the way she often screamed during the exorcism. It startled me so that the fright stayed with me for hours, and everybody made fun of me… About two or three weeks later I was in Klingenberg once more for an afternoon, because I had business close by. That way I had an opportunity to talk with Anneliese. Her boyfriend was there, too, and we had a very nice conversation. Finally I said to her, "I must tell you, you gave me a real scare last time. I couldn't shake it for days. How come you get so excited when the name of Fleischmann is mentioned?" And then suddenly she began to scream. For the first time I saw how she struggled against it, how she smiled, then her face contorted, she smiled again, her face contorted, she went on screaming, and she was barely able to say quickly in between, "Please, don't take it too hard, I can't help it." Peter and I were quite surprised that we were able to see so clearly what she was doing. I immediately gave an exorcism command, saying that she should be left alone, and it was over. She became quiet. She excused herself, and the two of them prayed for me, because they could see the matter had upset me so that I had become quite pale. That evening, while Father Renz was reciting the exorcism, the sixth bad spirit, by the name of Fleischmann, announced himself saying that he was the fallen priest of Ettleben who had killed a man. He gave many details, none of which I had mentioned in her presence. It has been maintained since that she must have read the chronicle, but I can prove that at the time in question

it was in the hands of the archivist in Wurzburg. All those details came from her spontaneously, and it was a surprise for me, a very great surprise. Anneliese herself was tremendously afraid of this particular demon.

Father Alt goes on to relate of his early experiences at the Ettleben parish house. There were noises of someone walking up and down the stairs, doors slamming, and of someone knocking. The housekeeper was aware of and heard these noises.

Dr. Kehler wrote a prescription for Tegretol for Anneliese on October 1, 1975.

October 1, 1975:

Lucifer: "The other one of that the village, where the curse took place, was an envious woman: that woman from your mother's village. (When asked if others were cursed, there was no answer). Today, no one believes any longer in the Immaculate Conception. The Church? At present, most believe it is only a community. The modernists are killing it evermore. We are hard at work at this, so it may be drawn, and we throw much poison into the Church, so it will be drawn. By now, those who believe in the Church and are faithful and believe in her are very few. The rosary, they do not think it is modern. Many believe that after life, everything is finished. They are very many, and they live accordingly, because they do not pray any longer. Sins reach Heaven: but the thing will not last long. The one of 1917 (the Virgin of Fatima) said it. But only a few have listened to her. Death, tribulations, and famine, O yes, they will come again!"

Anna maintained that the woman who cursed Anneliese was from her village of Lieblfing and a refugee from the war. She did it out of envy because she and Josef were relatively well off financially, while the woman was struggling to survive. Peter stated that the Michels attempted to pursue the issue but the lady in question had died.

October 6, 1975:

Judas: "Giving of Communion in the hand is my work."

Once again the demons made fun of the norms and rules of the Church. When it is in their interest to sow doubt or division, they are capable of appearing as staunch defenders of the Church's traditions. Until changes to the liturgy were implemented after Vatican II, priests only gave communion to the faithful on the tongue. A priest's hands are consecrated in the ceremony of ordination where the Bishop anoints them with holy chrism while saying the words of consecration. For many, the change to receiving in the hand showed a lack of reverence. For these reasons and others, many were not happy with this change. The evil spirits, aware of this polemic, used this argument to weaken obedience to the hierarchy. Although this matter may not be a critical one, it is necessary to remember that in the primitive Church, communion was received in the hand. The rebellious spirits used this issue to sow division knowing that there was no theological reason why the Church could not permit giving communion in the hand.

> Father Rodewyk (to Judas): "Now you too can get away. Anneliese, by now cannot stand it anymore, physically as well."
> Judas: "She must bear a little longer still because she was cursed and because he (the guardian angel) is near her, or else she would already have hung herself."

Often exorcists are asked if demons can kill a possessed person. The answer is they may wish to but the will of God prevents it. Thanks to the Holy Angels, the action of demons is limited.

> Lucifer to Father Alt: "In fact, the snotnose was cursed. She belongs to us. The one from … cursed her. She is no longer alive."
> Exorcist: "Is she down with you?"
> Lucifer: "No!"
> Lucifer: "I have to say everything. Therefore the snotnose has to pay for it."
> Exorcist: "You have to get out of her!"
> Lucifer: "I don't want out yet, because I have so much to say!"

Father Rodewyk and Father Habiger arrived after the October 6, 1975 session had begun. Father Habiger was quite disturbed by what he witnessed. He asked Father Rodewyk if the demons could kill Anneliese. Father Rodewyk stated that there was no record of this ever happening.

Father Alt offered on two occasions prior to October 31, 1975, to drive Bishop Stangl to Klingenberg to visit with Anneliese and witness an exorcism session. Later when the exorcism sessions no longer seemed to have any success, the Michels and Thea Hein wanted the Bishop to come to Klingenberg. Father Alt never witnessed Anneliese ask or demand that the Bishop visit Klingenberg.

Father Renz quizzed Anneliese on various issues. She stated that she still slept on the floor, but during the sessions if she tried to lie down she would be forced to sit up. She said she was tormented in various ways and suffered severe anxiety. It was painful when the sign of the cross was made over her. She said that studying was a real catastrophe. Sometimes she picked it up quickly and other times she could look at a page for hours and understand nothing because she was so beleaguered. This began in the tenth grade (1968-1969). It was like a condition of anxiety and despair. When mass and communion was brought up, something often seemed to hold her back. It was as though she wasn't supposed to go into the church, and when she did she would get sick and have to leave.

October 10, 1975:

> Judas: "First, let us torment her still!"
> Exorcist: "How much longer?"
> Judas: "When I have said everything, I will get out."

The demons, in this case as in others, sometimes speak of the date in which they will leave the body of the one they possess. These statements relative to dates are never certain. If true, it is the exception.

> Nero: "The snotnose was cursed by a woman. I will come out soon, there are many like the snotnose."
> Judas: "The bishops are so foolish to believe the theologians rather than the pope. This is the month of the rosary, but very few recite it, because the parish priests think it is not modern. They are so foolish! If they knew its importance! It is a strong weapon against Satan and against us. I have to say it, unfortunately many do not believe in it."

These edifying words from the condemned pertaining to spiritual and good things may surprise some. They may also deceive. Other times it is as if God forces them to speak the truth. In other cases they speak in a resigned manner as if there is nothing they can do against a superior force.

When Judas criticizes the Bishops, he is speaking of a period of more than two decades in which many clergy felt an inclination towards the modern world and the modernization of the Church. This eagerness brought many to accept the latest theories proposed by theologians to the Magisterium. The 1970's and 1980's were years where the traditional teachings of the Church encompassing every topic were questioned again and again. Judas and the other demons made reference to this situation.

> Nero: "Yes, you have to follow the message of Fatima! The encyclical Humanae Vitae is decisive, there is no other way! The whole Humanae Vitae."
> Lucifer: "If the message of the Virgin Mary at Fatima is not given due importance and Humanae Vitae respected, a new punishment will come."

On October 13, 1975 (anniversary date of the last apparition of the Blessed Virgin Mary in Fatima, Portugal 1917, and now feast day of Our Lady of Fatima), an important change occurred. In the past, Anneliese felt the presence of the Blessed Virgin, but on this day, Mary began to communicate with her directly. Mary instructed her to record what she was told and to communicate this to Father Renz. Everyone including Anneliese had their doubts as to the origin of these new messages or inspirations. Regardless of this, Anneliese now had a greater desire and need to pray.

The following references to Anneliese's diary are taken with permission, from Dr. Felicitas D. Goodman's book "The Exorcism of Anneliese Michel." Portions of Anneliese's diary were copied and given to Dr. Goodman by Father Renz. The location of Anneliese's diary is not known.

Anneliese's diary, October 13, 1975:

> Mother of God: "You will often receive inspirations of this kind from me from now on. Things will not always be easy for you. Tell this to Father Arnold. Remember, he

is to be your spiritual counselor."

In describing how she receives these inspirations or messages, Anneliese stated that she does not see or hear anything. She is made to understand. This mystical phenomenon is called "inner locutions." With regard to the demons, she said that they were using her voice and she is only a spectator.

Hitler and Cain introduce themselves on October 13, 1975.

Anneliese's diary, October 14, 1975:

Savior: "Stigmata."

Anneliese's diary, October 15, 1975:

Lucifer: "The snotnose blurt out everything! Now she also receives suggestions from that One (Virgin Mary). Of the kind of the snotnose, there are still so many. They were taken to the neurotic clinics. The one from… (Mrs. N…) is not crazy! She exaggerates, yes, but crazy… No! He (the Savior) allows this, yes, but the snotnose is saving many souls with this (Lucifer repeats this): We are five (in addition to him): Judas, Nero, Cain, and Hitler. Holy water should come back in the homes! Also the Crucifix should return to its place of honor in homes. By her order (the Virgin Mary), the five holy wounds should be venerated in a special manner. The Holy Face should be venerated! This is commanded by the Nazarene because it is so much disfigured by men! For this reason it should be venerated. The medal of the Holy Face should be venerated. This is ordered by the One who has power over Heaven and Hell. Also the image of the face of Jesus painted by Sister Faustina should be propagated. Where this image is found, many blessings will come, to our great ruin. The Nazarene and his Mother have commanded us to state this. It is very important to pray to St. Joseph, it is most important!"

Anneliese's diary, October 16, 1975:

Mother of God: "You are going to complete the work of Barbara Weigand."
Anneliese: I resist; I can't do that, I say: "She should look for somebody else."
Mother of God says (I am writing along) "The judgment day is very, very close. Pray as much as you can for your neighborhood, your kin, your friends and benefactors, for priests and laity, for politicians and the people."
Mother of God tells me once more that I would become entirely free in October. (She had said this before, a few days ago, but at that time, I thought that the inspiration was not genuine.)

The subject of a judgment comes up often:

"A new judgment day is coming, so there."
"What is it going to be like?"
"Terrible, worse than the last two."

"Where?"
"In Europe."
On another occasion the demons said: "There will be roaring and crashing. Everything will be destroyed, there will be no grub."

Anneliese's diary, October 17, 1975:

Mother of God: "I want the dissemination of Barbara Weigand's mission."

Anneliese's diary, October 17, 1975:

Lucifer: "I will deal with the snotnose until she cracks. She does not even realize this, because we have stopped it from above. That she faints continuously is our doing too."
Exorcist: "Why do you treat Anneliese this way?"
Lucifer: "Because we have to leave her soon, so the pigs (people) believed at once. I had permission. We have to come out this month. I am crouched inside her because she was cursed by a woman from ... The lady... it was really she who ordered it for me to do it! It happened in 1951! She was a resentful woman. Yes we have perverted her. The snotnose was often in bed and sick. We have done this too. We are the cause of many illnesses but no one sees this. Pray for the sick. Set one's life according to Him (Christ) then nothing can get lost! During exams I confused her. We tired her out. We are so interested in possessing her!"
Judas: "No one speaks any longer of us, especially the Rev. Parish Priests."

The psychology of the demons is very interesting. On the one hand they do not want to be spoken of, while on the other hand they have a very boastful nature. In one respect they know it is better if people do not believe in them, but as it unfolds, everything points to them being proud beings, and wanting to be admired. Although this may seem contradictory, in fact, it is not as they know that in an exorcism they have been discovered and don't have anything to lose by revealing themselves.

Father Renz had copies of Barbara Weigand's manuscripts and was well acquainted with them. On October 17, Father Renz brought a volume to Anneliese.

Anneliese's diary, October 18, 1975:

Mother of God made me understand this morning that I did not act properly. After breakfast I immediately started reading Barbara Weigand's book and I did not help with the housework. Too curious! Duty!

Anneliese's diary, October 20, 1975:

Savior: "There is still something that you must write down."
(Anneliese) "What is that?"
Savior: "What I told you last night."

Anneliese: "I did not want to write that down because I thought it was from Satan. Besides, my nature revolts against the idea. Savior demands that I obey, therefore I will write it down."
Savior: "You will become a great saint."
Anneliese: "I still did not want to believe it, and then the Savior, to prove that I had heard correctly, made me weep tears."

The state of possession endured with patience and love certainly works powerfully towards ones sanctification. Since enduring the possessed state is more challenging than voluntary ascetic acts, there is little doubt Anneliese sanctified herself in a heroic way by accepting these sufferings for the benefit of others.

Savior: "Every suffering, even the most commonplace, bears much fruit when it is united to my suffering."

Anneliese's diary, October 20, 1975:

Lucifer: "It will not be long before San Damiano will be recognized. There are people who do not believe I exist. They are my dear ones. Some no longer have a spark of faith. They belong to me. The churches are empty! Few go there. They are in bad shape. We will get out in the month of that one (Virgin Mary). Judas Iscariot will be the first to leave. Then the others will follow him. I will be the last to leave in October. We shall all leave.

In October we shall go somewhere else. In Lohr (neurological clinic) there are more of us hidden there. There, one goes neither forward nor backward. I would be much happier if I had the snotnose at Lohr. With this, it will be shown the power we have, and what power we have on the intellect and on the will of man. In her examination to qualify for university she wrote almost nothing. During the examination of German language we have blown in her ears for hours, telling her she was damned. The first manifestation was in the tenth grade. Judas did it. We were the cause of all her ailments. She received them from us: tuberculosis, the infection in her head, and the sickness in her throat.

We have continuously caused them to the end. We did not bring her to suicide. To be among the damned, this was our most wicked intent, the worst for her. With this you can fancy what power we have on the intellect and on the will of man. We have suggested to her that He (the Savior) said that she was damned. The last day of October we shall leave her all of a sudden. And how pleased you will be! You have the power to expel us! The majority do not make use of it. They are most dear to us."

Acknowledging the power a demon has not only over the intellect, but also over the will of the one possessed, may sound strange to theologians not specialized in the field of possession. Nevertheless, demons can directly influence the will without necessarily going through the intermediary of the intellect, as normally is the case with temptation. In the majority of temptations, the will is influenced by way of the elements of which intelligence is comprised: Memory, imagination and reason.

However, in one possessed, it can often happen that the demon acts directly on the will. In these cases, the possessed person does not have the strength to do anything, (to work, to pray etc.), but on the contrary feels, without knowing why, an intense impulse to hate, or break a crucifix, for example. The will of the possessed can ultimately resist this impulse, as not even the will of the possessed is totally nullified, unless in a trance.

> Anneliese's diary, October 21, 1975:
>
> One thing I must say, even if over and over again I had doubts concerning the origin of the inspirations. Recently I have a greater desire or need to pray. Mother of God tells me that I will become entirely free in October. She said this a few days ago, but at the time I thought the inspiration was not genuine.

> Anneliese's diary, October 22, 1975:
>
> Lucifer: "We shall soon leave her. The one up there is expelling us. We are damned eternally. We also want to go up there. We do not want to go out. We shall continue to torment the snotnose. She is under the protection of the one up there (Virgin Mary). The worst thing is that the doctrine of the Church is being falsified!"

As previously indicated, the demons' statements are a mixture of truth and falsehood. Here, when they say the doctrine of the Church is falsified, they are inducing doubts as to the way the Church was lead after the Second Vatican Council. They try to sow distrust with respect for the Church by using the excuse that many priests at that time were teaching new and strange doctrines contrary to faith and doctrine. They knew of these abuses and tried to sow doubt in the priests and those who held to the traditional teachings of the Church. This must have been confusing for Anneliese, her family and friends, who were not in agreement with many of the errors committed against the traditional faith of the Church during that period. Today when one looks back, the damage done by those shepherds who openly opposed the Magisterium in areas of theology, morality and the liturgy can clearly be seen. For this reason, the words of the demons made an impact on the people at that time.

> Father Renz: "Can we still save many souls with our prayers?"
> Lucifer: "Yes! Also the hardened ones, but then penance has to be done, with sacrifices and with perseverance! Specifically, you should adopt a way of living according to the Nazarene! Barbara Weigand preached this often. She did not do it willingly, yet she did it. There must be the will to continuously correct and better one self."

> Anneliese's diary, October 24, 1975:
>
> Savior: "You will suffer a great deal and do penance, even now. But your sufferings, your sadness and desperation, will help me save souls."

Lucifer: "You should preach more. By order of the One up there, you should warn people of the danger of a world without God. They have abandoned the One in whom they can find peace."

Fleischmann: "No priest should marry. He is a priest forever. It is the same for religious. They should remain faithful to their vocation. Today many are unfaithful."

In the following weeks, Anneliese carefully noted certain pages and underlined certain words of Barbara Weigand from the manuscripts. For example, the following lines touched the heart of Anneliese:

"Why are you worried that perhaps you underwent your sufferings for nothing? Let us suppose that no one will believe anything you say. You should know that your merit stays the same as if you had converted the entire world, remember that!

On another page: I have told you this morning that I will, over and over again, forgive doubt and anxiety, as indeed I have forgiven you, although you have begged me that I should take away your suffering. I do not because you should know that from the moment you gave me your consent, you surrendered to me. I have taken possession of you, not only of your spirit, but also of your body, so that I shall dwell in you despite all of your doubts, unless you commit a grave sin. You must know that if suffering is caused by other people, they mainly come from me, and it is my hand that shapes them so that they make you suffer." [31]

These words of Barbara Weigand were very important to Anneliese, as they could not be any more applicable and pertinent to her own thinking and situation. It is certain that Anneliese's sufferings came from the demons. It is also certain that the demons could not have acted without God permitting it. Ultimately, everything depends on God's will. If it had not been God's will, the rebellious angels would not have been able to approach her. So why would God allow such great suffering? The reason appears again and again in the writings of all spiritual writers since the beginning of the Church two thousand years ago: suffering accepted with love for God transforms the soul. In other words, to crucify one with Christ is terrible for the body and is a Calvary for the soul, but the spirit of that person is filled with love for God to the point that it is impossible for those who have not experienced total surrender to the divine will to understand. Essentially, this theological reality is what explains the phenomena surrounding the possession of Anneliese, as well as the sufferings of all holy souls in the world.

Anneliese's diary, October 27, 1975:

Fleischmann: "Communion in the hand should be abolished. This is our work. The Bishop should forbid Communion in the hand, if he had already permitted it. I have a message from the one who cursed the snotnose. You have to pray for her. She is down there, in the deepest purgatory."

Lucifer: "It is quite a time that Bishop (Rudolf) Graber of Ratisbon is a thorn in my eye. The apparitions at San Damiano and Montechiari are true. The church did not recognize them, but this is our work."

The apparitions of San Damiano and Montechiari are summarized in the Appendix.

Anneliese's diary, October 27, 1975:

"The Savior promised me that I would come out of this suffering purer and I would not fall."

Anneliese's diary, October 29, 1975:

"If I am not mistaken, Barbara Weigand said to me yesterday afternoon I would have to suffer a great deal."

Diary undated: The nephew of Father Roth (Siegfried, paralyzed since childhood, who had died the week before) was here with me on the evening of October 10 and let me know he was in heaven. I did not want to believe this at first. I did come around to believing it. First because he came to me this morning and several times during the day (as far as seeing is concerned, I see nothing) and secondly because he always tries to give me courage. When I asked him why he visited me so often, he said it was because I also had to suffer, as he suffered when he was alive. He promised to give me support in all my tribulations.

Anneliese's diary, October 29, 1975:

Mother of God: "Later you will also have visions." If I understood correctly, as compensation for the satanic countenances that I saw in the past and those I still see. I am not sure if this was something Satan deluded me with.

Mystical visions and locutions are the fruit of the cross and its suffering. Some of the possessed have suffered so much and at the same time have submitted so perfectly to God's will, leading an intense life of prayer and sacrifice, that they have begun to experience the phenomena of the mystical life without having been freed from their possession. There are several cases like this throughout history, of long enduring possessions, experienced together with mysticism. One may ask how it is possible for a person to be possessed and at the same time enjoy intense union with God. The answer is simple. The demon is in the body and the soul is united to God while bearing this cross of possession. This is the reason why Holy Communion can be given to a possessed person during exorcism if the person is in a state of grace to receive the sacrament. The demon does not necessarily leave even when the person receives Holy Communion, because God permits the person's sufferings for its sanctification and the good of the Church. This cross of the possessed person will gain many graces for other souls. There are possessed persons who undergo the cross of not knowing if the visions they receive are from God or the demon. This person requires good spiritual direction and must be obedient to this direction.

Anneliese's diary, October 29, 1975:

I must confess that when I thought of Father Herrmann and Father Habiger, I often felt resentment against them, because in 1973 they would not believe Satan was molesting and tormenting me. Last night the Savior let me feel that the priests did the right thing, because at the time they had no visible proof. Only Thea Hein and Father Alt had this proof. The Black One always sneaked off.

Anneliese's diary October 29, 1975:

The Black One (Fleischmann) threatened me with his fist.
Savior: "You will come to see why I demand this of you."

Anneliese's diary, October 29, 1975:

Mother of God during exorcism: "On Friday I will come and chase them away."

In cases where a person has suffered possession for a long period while living a spiritual and sacramental life, it may happen that an angel speaks through them while in a trance. In many cases this is reasonable to believe, not only because of the edifying comments which are being made or the majestic tone of the voice which is speaking, but also because of the fact that sometimes the angel gives the command for the demon to leave and the demon actually leaves. Therefore, the diary entries are not out of the ordinary in spite of what some may think. Possessions and the process of exorcism are the way they are and not the way people expect them to be.

On October 31, 1975, Dr. Kehler wrote out a prescription for Tegretol.

The anticipated session on October 31, 1975 finally arrived. Earlier in the day, Father Rodewyk wished them good luck and warned them that even after the demons have been expelled, there is a risk of them returning. It was a long session. There were prayers to the Blessed Virgin Mary, guardian angel, the souls in purgatory, Barbara Weigand, and the Holy Spirit, to name a few. Upon questioning, it was revealed that the Blessed Virgin Mary, St. Joseph, Padre Pio, Martha, Siegfried, Anneliese's grandmothers, Theresa Neumann, and St. Michael etc. were present. The demons stated: "It is hard to be in this room, there are so many holy people present." [32] The presence of demons inside the body of a person with an intense spiritual life is torture for the demons.

During this session, each of the demons seemed to be driven out. First Fleischmann, then Hitler, Cain, Nero, Judas, and lastly Lucifer. Each as their turn came, after retching, screaming and of sounds indescribable, they repeated Hail Mary full of grace and then remained silent. Father Alt stated, "We felt an unspeakable relief, an amazing relief." Anneliese said, "I am completely free, now completely free." [33] After about fifteen minutes, the closing hymn was interrupted by a horrific guttural growl and scream. "I have not gone out yet." Father Renz asked who had not gone yet. The response was that he was one who had not previously revealed his presence. Euphoric joy had turned to despair as they all realized the demons were again present. After laboring further to expel the demons, Father Renz concluded the evening session at about 1:30 am; a much longer session than usual.

Although Anneliese was feeling better, everyone involved was deeply disappointed. The next session was held on November 3, with no success. Anneliese went to Wurzburg the next day as she had to prepare for an exam. She found it hard to study. For the time being, it was easy for her to pray and she preferred to pray. At times she would pray for several hours at a time. A few days before her exam, she was able to cram. She received a good grade in spite of a demons comment during the November 3 session that she was not going to pass her exam. Also, for the first time in a while, she was able to go to mass and confession. In the past when attending mass, when communion came, she became stiff and couldn't move to receive.

Anneliese's diary, November 3, 1975:

Judas: "We shall not go. Our business will take some time yet. We have deceived you. We will not get out. Today the dirty slut went to church. Stop with that thing (pointing to the exorcist). We shall not come out yet. We are going to torment the snotnose for some time yet. She doesn't know anything, and cannot take her examinations. Last Friday we exhausted the snotnose."

Anneliese's diary, November 8, 1975:

> Judas: "I am eternally damned. I am here for some time yet. Do not always call me by name."

It is necessary to state that a human soul condemned to hell is like a demon who speaks during a possession. Although condemned human souls do not become demons, they are like demons. The different natures of humans and angels remain different whether they are saved or condemned. A human will never become an angel if saved, or will never become a demon if condemned.

> Present: Lucifer, Cain, Hitler, Nero, and Fleischmann etc. ten in total.
> "By order of the High Dame, be patient."

Anneliese's diary, November 8, 1975:

> Savior: "I was glad you came to see me; quite often there is no one here." I am to visit him more often when I am in Wurzburg, and I am to take Anna (Lippert) with me.

Anneliese's diary, November 9, 1975:

> Judas: "The one from Schippach (Barbara Weigand) is the right person for the renewal."

Anneliese's diary, November 10, 1975:

Savior: "You will pass all your tests (my teacher's examinations). But you are going to be called upon to undergo tests of a different kind. I will give you my grace. You will be true unto death."

The following was taken from four notebooks given by Anneliese to Father Renz. She didn't indicate where these notes came from. [34]

1. Everything you do well, or have done well in the past is from Me, every good thought, every good deed. Nothing is from you. This is why I let you oversleep (late for holy mass) in order to show you that you are not able to do anything by yourself, and in order to humiliate you. You are not to believe you have accomplished anything. Everything is a gift of My love for you.
2. Expect everything from Me, everything. I can make the impossible, possible. Trust me completely. This honors Me. It attracts Me.
3. Repent of your sins and believe I have forgiven you and go on courageously. Believe in My great love for you, do not doubt it as this makes Me very sad. My ways are mysterious ways. You will have to leave it to Me what path I choose for you. Have I not given you many tokens of My love?
4. Be silent! Do not speak so much. Keep a tight rein over your tongue. For you will have to give an accounting of every superfluous word. Love loneliness. Go to social affairs only if it is necessary to show your loyalty to others, not for the sake of pleasure. Also, renounce permitted pleasures.
5. Do not worry about the future. Unburden everything on Me. Seek every minute you can to listen to Me, to fulfill My will, My slightest wish, by listening to My voice. The lambs know the voice of their shepherd. I am the good shepherd and I love My lambs.
6. Believe that I grant every prayer if it does not stand in the way of the salvation of the soul. Often I do not grant the legitimate requests of My children for a long time in order to make them steadfast.
7. Do not become upset immediately if things do not right away turn out as you would like. At least try to govern your temper. You do not know what a vexation may be good and useful for. You should be grateful for it. Often I do not grant even legitimate requests to my children, in order to make them steadfast and to let their prayers benefit some sinner. Be patient toward the lack of faith of other people, as I am patient with you. The patient person and the steadfast one accomplish everything which is essential.
8. Pray and plead incessantly for your fellow human beings so that they may also reach their heavenly home.
9. Am I not a loving father who takes care of you?
10. Do not forget what a gift of grace it is that you are permitted to read the writings of Barbara Weigand. Pray that soon the treasury of these writings may be made available to everyone.
11. Pray and make many sacrifices for my priests. Not for nothing did I show you the greatness and dignity of every priest (in San Damiano) so that you shuddered with awe. Consider that even the most unworthy priest is a second Christ. Do not judge anyone so that you will not be judged. Leave that to me.
12. Struggle against temptation and do not surrender. I will not allow it to exceed

your strength. How far I will allow temptation to come your way need not concern you. That is up to me. One grows with struggle if you struggle with Me.

Paragraph twelve (12.) is important. It is not the same to fight with one's own will, as with the aid of the sacraments, knowing one fights against desperation, accompanied by Christ.

The sessions on November 10, 16, 17 and 23, 1975 were uneventful. In between trips home, Anneliese was working in Wurzburg on her thesis.

On November 23, the demon stated that he and the others were not going to stop pestering the snotnose. He said; *"The exalted Lady is here."* After some prodding, he revealed Padre Pio, Barbara Weigand, Anneliese's grandmother, St. Joseph, guardian angels and others were also present.

Anneliese's diary, November 24, 1975:

Judas: "What a pity the synod has ended. It has given us great joy!"

Here is another criticism against the Church in Germany. The commentary sympathizes with the traditionalists. The situation at this time was of doctrinal chaos. Just because Judas states this, it should not be dismissed as false. Again, at this time, the eagerness to modernize caused some to set aside some of the teachings and liturgical norms held for centuries.

Anneliese was feeling better and continued to study for her exams. On November 27, she received the 'Missio Canonica': the church's certification to teach religion.

During the November 28, 1975 session, the demon revealed that Anneliese had written an exam the previous day with the help of the Blessed Virgin Mary and Theresa Neumann. The demon again addressed the German Bishops conference, stating his approval of the reforms made.

The sessions continued on December 7, 12, 14, 19 and 30, 1975.

On December 1 Dr. Kehler wrote a prescription for Tegretol. December 7 was the first session Gertraud was present. The demon argued that there was no afterlife and Jesus never lived. "You should know" was Father Renz's response. Father Renz appealed to Theresa Neumann for her intercession on behalf of Anneliese. After this session, Anneliese indicated that she felt better and wished to receive Holy Communion. Peter drove Father Renz and Anneliese to the church in Schippach where Anneliese received Holy Communion.

Anneliese's diary, December 12, 1975:

Lucifer: "If that one goes once more (to Communion), I will tear her to pieces. I will spit out that thing (the host). And to make things worse, she also kneels down, the stupid sow!"

Anneliese's diary, December 19, 1975:

Exorcist: "Where is Fleischmann?"
Judas: "He is away but he may still come back… and there are still many more here, and you know absolutely nothing. We too want to go up there (Heaven). We are damned eternally! Out! Out! We wish to come out of the snotnose. We cannot bear staying in her any longer. That filthy slut stays the whole day in the church. We are damned! Damned!"
Exorcist: "Then come out!"
Judas: "We cannot, because He does not allow it. The one up there, that one does not want it! He wants us to remain. We want to get out from that one, who goes to Communion, and she goes every day! We cannot bear this! We wish to come out, out, out! And she even kneels down. We wish to come out, but the one up there does not allow us!"
Exorcist: "Why does He not allow you?"
Judas: "Ha! Because, ha! Because? We wish to come out, out, out! Stop praying! We are damned, damned, damned! We want to come out we are damned, damned for eternity! [On the tape there is a dreadful emphasis on the words damned and eternity.] Do you know what that one knew at the examination! This is inconceivable! She deserves a mark of three. She will infallibly pass the next examination. It is He, up there who permitted it, thus the exorcism takes place."

Since the beginning of the year, the sessions had become shorter and less eventful. It was more difficult to engage the demons. Father Renz continued to come once or twice a week. For exorcism sessions to extend for months and even years is common. There may be periods where nothing happens. This can be demoralizing for an exorcist. In these cases the priest may feel the impotence of not being able to cause the demon to leave or even have it speak. Father Renz and Father Alt went through this desert.

Anneliese's diary, January 6, 1976:

Exorcist: "Why can you not come out?"
Judas: "We do not know the reason."

Anneliese's diary, January 22, 1976:

Judas: "Lucifer is not pleased with the one (Anneliese) who has copied the writings of Weigand, and I too do not like it. It is certain the powers of darkness will become more powerful. Also this is written inside, and this is true. And it is also true that men will take the places which were left vacant up there (by fallen angels), and we can torment them. In this century there will be as many saints as never before. However, many also come down here with us, and people do not believe. They all believe all is well with them and they provide every comfort for themselves. If they knew! But then, when they will realize it, it will be too late… then, no one will ever come back…!"

The repeated reference to San Damiano and Barbara Weigand by the demons lessens the credibility of the reality of what the demon speaks because it seems they are promoting propaganda for this place of pilgrimage and that of the mystic. In spite of this, it is common in cases of possession which last a long time for the demons to refer to a saint or a particular message.

> Anneliese's diary, January 23, 1976:
>
> Father Renz: "You are responsible for heresies, for example those of Kung!"
> Lucifer: "Yes, and we have still more."
> Father Renz: "And Bishop Lefebvre?"
> Lucifer: "Ha, that one! But they do not believe in him. What a pity!"

The words which lament that more people do not follow the schismatic Bishop Lefebvre should be looked at carefully. They try to lead the faithful astray through liberal theologians as well as traditional theologians. Bishop Marcel Lefebvre, who was considered a traditionalist, was excommunicated for disobedience, not theological error. The goal of the demons is always to draw the faithful away from the teachings of the Church and from obedience to the Church. They do not mind being champions of orthodoxy and tradition, or heroes of modernism and being with the times, whichever helps attain their goal. These kinds of conversations are common in exorcisms. A general rule is to avoid questions of curiosity and stick to questions which directly relate to the expelling the demons. Bishop Lefebvre was well known for his traditional views while Hans Kung was known for challenging many teachings of Catholic faith (Papal infallibility). Kung's license to teach in Catholic universities was revoked in 1979.

> Exorcist: "Is she doing what you wish?"
> Judas: "No! But sometimes yes. All do this, as well as those who will take their place above. He permits it so they do not become proud. Why should I say this? It is also written in the Scriptures."
> Exorcist: "Should you cooperate to foster the love of God?"
> Judas: "Yes, so it is! And this is a frightful thing."

When the exorcisms began, the demons and those condemned were conscious of the fact that by participating and speaking during the exorcism sessions they risked increasing the faith of those involved. This would cause great suffering for them because their only goal is to separate souls from God.

> Anneliese's diary, February 1, 1976:
>
> Judas: "Next week, the snotnose will not eat. She has to fast, that stupid slut! We still want to torment her, and it is useful to fast. After all, she will not die of starvation! For the exams she can eat. But she knows really nothing, really nothing. If she followed our advice, she would not have studied. We have always worked against her, we have always been present. But the One above does it. He does it step by step."
> Exorcist: "And what profit do you draw in tormenting Anneliese?"

Judas: "It is our amusement! There is only wickedness and torment in us. We wish to come out!"
Exorcist: "Then get out if you wish it!"
Judas: "It is useless, we have lost her! O, terror! She cannot guess it! Yes, here too a fire is burning, but worse, much wars (in hell)."

Continuation of February 1, 1976, conversation Father Renz had with Anneliese:

"The other problem that I had all week is I was not permitted to eat, or I could eat only very little. One day I was not allowed to eat at all."

"How did you know that?"

"I feel it. I may be tremendously hungry, and then there is a barrier there, it is like a compulsion, and I am not allowed to… What also happened was that I was not allowed to put on any gloves or a cap, and it was cold outside. It wouldn't be so bad, but when the weather gets as cold as it did last week, it sure makes me shiver. And during the night I was not allowed to cover myself properly."

"And he also demanded other things, didn't he?"

"The worst of it was that I had to get undressed completely, even though it lasted only one and a half hours. And the terrible compulsion that I am supposed to go to Anna (Lippert). You have to do it with an urgency you cannot imagine what it is like Father. I cannot explain how that was. Suddenly it was gone. I pleaded: Lord my Savior, I cannot do that, and Lord it is not possible. It did not help one bit. I have found that I can storm the heavens all I want. They are deaf."

"Perhaps you were thinking about what he said, that he was going to torment those who were slated to assume places in heaven?"

"I don't know whether I did. Oh, Father, I never thought it would be as cruel as this. I always thought I would want to suffer for others so they would not have to go to hell, but I did not realize it could be this bad and this cruel and terrible. People think suffering is an easy matter, but when things get really awful you don't want to go on, you don't want to take a single step further."

"I am feeling quite well now, but as for Communion, I am trying to go, I try to get up, but it just isn't possible. Father Arnold, it is really difficult to imagine what that is like. How is it possible that they can force a person like this? You have no power of your own at all. I don't understand at all how something like that is possible."

"To feel that you are completely delivered up to evil, to its power?"

"Yes, something like that."

"But just think, he has only power over your body. It is when the evil one has power over one's soul that is when things are really bad. You can't do anything against it as you are being forced, so you carry no responsibility."

"I did not feel that I was damned. No, I did not think so. That would have been worse."

"I have to pray a great deal. There is such a contradiction here. I do it voluntarily, and yet there is pressure behind it. It was also that way this past summer. Sometimes I could not pray for days and weeks. At other times I had to kneel for hours and pray one rosary after another until twelve or one o'clock at night, and papa prayed with me. I was forced to do it. It was terrifying. I felt an abysmal horror no one can imagine that… That horror may have had something to do with the fact that I wanted to have nothing to do with sacred things."

"Not with the picture of the Savior either?"

"Right. Because I connected these things, because He allowed it, that things became so cruel." [35]

The terrible thing about possession is not only the possession of the body but also the demons' influence on the mind. They may introduce insistent impulses towards obsessions, fear and desperation. From this perspective it is necessary to understand the obsessive repetition of genuflexions and prayers Anneliese had in the final stage of her possession.

Anneliese's diary, February 8, 1976:

When Father Renz was imposing a scapular on Anneliese and commanding the evil spirits to leave her at once, Judas responded: "We cannot, so soon, still not so soon. It will be in the summer."

Anneliese's diary, February 13, 1976:

Judas: "We are damned! Your mother is now out of purgatory and we are crushed down there. You, you are all like that one."
Exorcist: "You have to leave!"
Judas: "We cannot! Only when the High Dame and He (Savior) want it! It will not be too long from now!"

Anneliese's diary, February 15, 1976:

Savior: "Pray and intercede without interruption for your neighbor so they may reach the eternal Motherland! Pray and offer much for my priests. For some reason I have showed you the greatness and dignity of every priest, so much so, that you were frightened. Keep in mind that even an unworthy priest is another Christ. To avoid judgment, do not judge anyone. Leave this task to me."

Anneliese's diary, February 20, 1976:

Judas: "We wish to get out."
Exorcist: "Then why do you not get out?"
Judas: "We wish to get out of hell and from that one (Anneliese), out of both of them."

The body of the possessed becomes a jail for the evil spirits. Anneliese was like a city surrounded by her exorcists and those who helped them in this spiritual battle. Even though it was spiritual, it was a real battle. Anneliese was like a fortress where the demons remained on the defensive from their attackers, while at the same time the fortress was a jail for the occupants. On the one hand, they wanted to get out because they did not feel well inside, but on the other hand they resisted because if they left the body they would not likely return.

Anneliese's diary, February 23, 1976:

Judas: "We are damned, damned, damned! We want to get out!"
Exorcist: "Why are you damned? Why have you kissed the Lord?"
Judas: "Because I fell into despair!"
Exorcist: "You cannot stay here long."
Judas: "If you know so much, there is no need for me to say anything more."
Exorcist: "Will it be this week?"
Judas: "No, I should not tell you!"
Exorcist: "When can Anneliese go to Communion?"
Judas: "The snotnose cannot go, only the One on the cross will allow her to go to Communion. During Mardigras (carnival) we are set free. We still have to deal with the snotnose, do you understand? Yes, tonight I will torment her as she deserves."
Exorcist: "I forbid you to do so!"
Judas: "No, because I will trample upon the stupid sow. She had no peace for the whole night! It is Mardigras and the High Dame needs reparation and substitution for others who will dance with me the whole night. Yes, I am after her…"
Exorcist: "She is under the protection of the Virgin Mary."
Judas: "Yes, but she is a person. She will not make noise externally the thing could go also otherwise…"
Exorcist: "Who are you?"
Judas: "We are damned, we are damned!"

From February 29, 1976 on, the demons had nothing more to say. They only raved and roared; they made mindless inhuman sounds as Anneliese's body jerked like a rag doll.

Chapter VII

ANNELIESE'S LAST DAYS

On Ash Wednesday, March 3, 1976, Anneliese traveled to Wurzburg. She was unable to return home for the weekend because her body became stiff and she was quite ill. Her friends found her on the floor in her room in a crouched position. A few hours later, Peter called the Michels as Anneliese was not able to pick up the phone. Anna, Josef and Roswitha came to visit her. Roswitha stayed to help care for Anneliese. When Father Renz arrived, he found her barely conscious and received virtually no response to his exorcism prayers. Anneliese said the prayers made her feel better and she spoke of the demons quarreling among themselves.

Anneliese's condition improved so she continued working on her thesis. A few days later, another attempt to travel to Klingenberg failed when her body became stiff and she was unable to move. She contacted Thea Hein. Thea picked her up at the train station in Sulzbach, and during lunch at the Heins', Anneliese revealed the purpose of her visit. She told Thea that she wouldn't get up off her knees until Thea promised to protect her and never allow anyone to call a doctor. She stated that the medicine did not help and only prayer gave her relief. After Thea promised to do everything within her power, they drove back to the train station. On the way, Anneliese alerted Thea that a horrid smell was coming. She immediately stopped the car and they got out for ten minutes, as they could not stand the smell.

Anneliese had a deep fear of being found mentally unstable and sent to a mental institution. She had foreseen this danger for a long time. A stay in such a hospital might make it difficult for her to get a teaching position. This danger had increased as Judas announced that her condition was going to get worse. The demons admitted it was their desire to have Anneliese in a mental institution. There, she would not have the benefit of the exorcism prayers and may perhaps die there, out of the public view where the world would not have been aware of her possession and sufferings.

In April, Anneliese told Father Alt that May and June were going to be tough months, but July would bring a resolution to her condition. On Tuesday of Holy

Week, Anneliese felt drawn to the chapel at Ferdinandeum. After a period of prayer she attempted to leave. She kept involuntarily falling back onto her knees to the point where her knees began to bleed. It was the next morning before she was able to leave.

On April 14 Anneliese went to see Dr. Veth to discuss her thesis. Dr. Veth later explained to the criminal investigator the following:

> "It was my impression that Miss Michel dedicated herself to her work with a great deal of industry and personal involvement. From her critical statements concerning some of the publications on her topic, I gained the impression that she had a lucid ability to judge the data, and she was definitely determined to conclude the third part of her thesis as quickly as possible…As far as her psychological and physical condition during the interview was concerned, I saw nothing whatsoever to worry about." [36]

On Holy Thursday evening, Anneliese went to the church of Our Lady to pray. She had barely begun to pray when she broke out in a heavy sweat that soaked her clothes. It was late before she was able to return to her room. Anneliese felt as if something weighed on her and she spent the night on the floor unable to sleep. She spent Good Friday morning in prayer before the altar in her room. At 3:00 pm, she went back to the church for Good Friday services. After Good Friday services were over, she remained in the church. Several hours later, Mechthild found her standing, eyes closed, holding her prayer book in a trance-like state. Later, she returned with Peter and found Anneliese in the same position. Anneliese didn't respond to Peter's questions. He told her he would stay and pray for her. It wasn't until late in the evening that Anneliese was able to move. On the way home, she explained to Peter everything that had happened and told him that she now had an idea of what Jesus suffered during his passion.

The next day, Anneliese was exhausted. Her body became stiff and she had to be helped into bed. She remained in this unconscious or semi-conscious state for almost two weeks. Anna Lippert was the only one in Anneliese's group of friends who was aware of the extent and nature of Anneliese's suffering.

During the evening of April 30, 1976, Anneliese began to scream loudly and continuously. Roswitha and Anna were worried that she might be heard by others in the building. They called Father Renz requesting an exorcism. Father Alt was also called, and he promised to come the following morning.

The next morning, Peter found Anneliese relaxed as if nothing had happened. When Father Alt arrived, he suggested contacting Dr. Veth and informing him of what was happening. This was done. It was decided that due to the circumstances, Anneliese couldn't stay there any longer. There was a room at the parish house in Ettleben where Anneliese could work on her thesis in quiet and Father Alt would be close by, if needed. During the drive to Ettleben, Anneliese told Peter that she would have to suffer until July.

At the beginning of her stay in Ettleben, Anneliese began to eat and drink and was in good cheer. This did not last for long. She began to moan and scream for hours on end. She could not eat and slept on the floor with her body stiff and contorted. Roswitha and a lady from the village came to help. One night Roswitha found Anneliese half out of bed gasping for air. She indicated that she was being choked.

While in Ettleben, Anneliese wanted to see the renovations to the church. Shortly after entering the church her face became contorted. She indicated to Peter that she would have to remain and pray until the beginning of the evening mass. When Peter attempted to pick Anneliese up from the pew, she was so heavy he could not move her (possessed gravity). Only after Father Alt came and prayed over her were they able to return to the house.

During Anneliese's stay at Ettleben, the demonic attacks continued. Father Alt tried to comfort her by telling her that it would not last much longer. In February, Anneliese told Father Alt she was so tired that she had no energy to continue. Father Alt counseled her that she must do what God wanted. Anneliese's response was that although she was tired, she would go on. At Ettleben in April, Anneliese stated very seriously to Father Alt: "I know now what will happen, I know this coming summer will be hard and terrible and I know I will not survive. No one can tell me any different. I will not survive." [37]

In spite of all her terrible suffering, her faith remained unshaken. When the demons left her free, she was cheerful and would laugh and joke as if nothing had happened. For those who were with her, this was a deeply moving experience.

After being in Ettleben for a week, it was decided that Anneliese should return to Klingenberg. On May 9, 1976, Josef, Anna, Peter and Barbara came to drive her home. She stiffened and became so heavy that several men could barely lift her into the car.

As Anneliese had indicated, the months of May and June were going to be bad, but there would be a turn in July. She was fearful and sad not knowing exactly what was ahead of her. One minute she might be her normal self, the next she would be wild. She slept very little and often was unable to eat. Pictures of her at this time show her emaciated and her eyes black and blue. She injured herself in various ways. She would hit her head against objects, punch her face, bite herself, and rub her face against the wall. On a couple of occasions, she asked to be tied up to minimize her injuries.

Anna described how Anneliese appeared to be continuously thrown to the ground, on her back. She would often hit her head. It went on for hours that she would get up and seem to be thrown down again. Through this whole ordeal Anneliese prayed, "Hail Mary full of grace…" Not knowing what else to do, Anna called the priests. As Anneliese was unable to protect herself, Anna placed pillows and quilts on the floor. In spite of this, Anneliese's head and face were black and blue and her eyes were swollen. [38]

Unlike previously, the demons and Anneliese had nothing to say during the sessions of May 10, 12, 14 and 17. She didn't react to the exorcism prayers although she was aware of all that was going on.

The deadline for Anneliese's thesis was again extended. She recovered to the extent that she was able to dictate the balance of her paper to Peter and her sisters. Only after her family said a rosary for her, was she able to muster the strength to sign her paper. It was completed on May 28, 1976.

The following are two quotes from her thesis:

> "Let it here be noted, that Jesus did not heal all the sick. As to the question of why, it can only be said that for God, it all depends on the state of the soul of the person. Someone who is capable and willing to bear suffering and from whom God does not take it away, in the end, will achieve more for himself than if he had never had to bear the suffering." [39]

> "In conclusion, let it be said that there exists, cases where someone, even though he has confessed and lives interiorly at peace with God, nevertheless is troubled by a significant anxiety, from an anxiety of body and of death, from which one may not free himself. When this is experienced by someone, one can only silently stand by and pray that he will be brought through this period of anxiety. There exists a particular sharing of the Cross of Christ and his death agony. The most important attitude is to have a pastoral and medical care, a reverence before the mystery of a man's life with God." [40]

On May 30, 1976, Dr. Richard Roth, a friend of Father Alt, came to witness one of the exorcism sessions. Dr. Roth had listened to some of the exorcism tapes and told Father Alt the tapes had prompted him to pray again. Dr. Roth was curious to see the events for himself, while Father Alt was glad to have a doctor present at a time when Anneliese's condition had worsened. Several days before, Anneliese had chipped her teeth after biting the wall and her face was quite bruised and swollen. Her level of arousal was such that Father Alt suggested to Dr. Roth he give Anneliese something to calm her down. Father Alt witnessed his friend put some ampules and a syringe in his pocket prior to entering the house. Upon seeing Anneliese, Dr. Roth exclaimed: "My God, she has the stigmata!" He suggested no physician could do anything in this case. He was quoted as saying: "There is no injection against the devil." He stated that this was the first time he had witnessed someone possessed and that he could not treat her as he did not know how she would react to the medication. Later, under oath, Dr. Roth stated that he did not remember saying this and that he was present as a spectator, not as a physician. After the session, they all went to the living room for coffee and cake and discussed Anneliese's condition. At Josef's request, Dr. Roth wrote on two occasions, a certificate stating that Anneliese could not work for two weeks which would allow her to postpone her student teaching. This would bring them closer to the much hoped for resolution in July.

Father Alt came again on June 8, 1976. Her face was sunken and she looked very ill. When Father Alt asked what Anneliese was eating he was told she sometimes was able to eat a banana. There were times however when Anneliese would suddenly blurt out "Give me something to eat!" She would eat very quickly and the last bites she could not swallow and had to spit out. It seemed that once in a while she had a brief window of time in which she could eat or drink. Sometimes she would drink two litres

of juice.[41] June 8th was the last time Father Alt saw Anneliese alive. He wrote to the Bishop on June 24, 1976, wherein he described her self-inflicted injuries and how she had bitten a hole in the wall and chipped her teeth. As a result of Anneliese having gone through a glass door, her left eye was swollen shut. She ate little or nothing. He suggested that this was a case of "penance possession" whereby she had to suffer for the sins of another, perhaps someone in her family. For Father Alt, the fact that the demons no longer spoke was an indication they were dealing with a penance possession. Anneliese stated that things were going to get worse. She was very afraid. Father Alt said the only consolation was that many souls would be saved through her sufferings.

On June 2, Father Renz reported to the Bishop. He described her injuries, and that her face was black and blue from hitting herself. She had suffered grievously the previous few days and her family was close to despair. He mentioned that Anneliese had asked to have her hands and feet tied. Father Renz continued the sessions on June 9. Amongst agonizing screams, Anneliese's only words were "Absolution" and "I can't go on." Although the demons did not speak, their raging and screaming was particularly terrifying. Sometimes they screamed all night. In his last letter to the Bishop dated June 20, 1976, Father Renz stated that some of Anneliese's injuries had healed excepting her nose and knee. She made countless genuflections, up to 600 at a time without stopping. She ate and drank little and looked emaciated. Anneliese stated repeatedly to those concerned for her that she would gladly eat except the demons wouldn't allow her.

Amidst the terror and pain Anneliese experienced at this time, there were periods where she spoke normally with Peter and her family. Peter stated that Anneliese was always absolutely clear in her decisions. The two topics most discussed were the hope that all would be over in July and whether they should seek medical help. Anneliese always refused the latter.

On June 27, Anneliese had a fever of 39.9 degrees C. This was brought down by cold compresses. Josef called Father Alt who suggested calling a doctor. When Roswitha asked Anneliese, she refused. The following day she had nothing to eat or drink. In addition, she was compelled to make countless genuflections.

At the last exorcism session on June 30, 1976, Josef, Anna, Roswitha, Barbara and Peter were present. Father Renz prayed the exorcism prayers. Her temperature was again around 39 degrees C. Anneliese suddenly asked: "Please, absolution." Father Renz immediately complied. These were the last words spoken to Father Renz. Peter and Josef held Anneliese and Anna used a pillow to mitigate the repeated genuflections she insisted on making. After Father Renz and Peter said their goodbyes, Anneliese asked her mother to stay.

Her last words were:

"Mama, please stay with me. I'm afraid."

It was past midnight, the first day of July 1976. When Josef checked on Anneliese at 7:00 am, he thought she was asleep.

At 8:00 am, Anna called Josef to tell him that Anneliese was dead.

No one ever imagined, even during the preceding days, that the outcome could be as transpired.

During the last days, all were hanging on Anneliese's words, that on July 1 she would be free of the demons. Anneliese and Peter had talked about getting married in the fall.

She was now indeed free.

Chapter VIII

THE TRIAL

On the morning of July 1, 1976, Anna called Father Alt to inform him that Anneliese had died during the night. Father Alt could not believe it. He called Dr. Roth, who agreed to be available in case of a medical emergency. He asked Dr. Roth to drive to Klingenberg as soon as possible to investigate the situation as he believed Anneliese was in a trance or in ecstasy. Dr. Roth arrived from Frankfurt shortly after noon and immediately called Father Alt to confirm Anneliese's death. He estimated the time of death to be 6:00 am. He would have filled out a death certificate but he did not have the proper forms with him. Dr. Martin Kehler was called. He inspected the body and found it emaciated and still warm. He didn't issue a death certificate because he could not state that Anneliese's death was due to natural causes. A postmortem showed the cause of death was due to starvation, possibly aggravated by physical exertion. Her internal organs, including her brain, were healthy. Her pupils were dilated and there were no bedsores commonly present on persons who starved to death. A criminal investigation began. It is interesting to note, that if Dr. Roth had brought the proper papers for a death certificate with him, it is possible that this case may never have become known.

The following is a letter signed by District Attorney Stenger dated July 1, 1976: [42]

> "Today, at half past one, I had a telephone call from a Father Alt. He did not give his address. He described a case of exorcism (driving out of devils) to me, which he said he had carried out on a young girl by the name of Anneliese Michel of Klingenberg. He described previous treatments the girl had undergone, all without success, by psychiatrists and neurologists in Aschaffenburg, specifically Dr. Siegfried Luthy in Wurzburg. He described the symptoms she had been suffering from and the successes and failures of the exorcism. He mentioned that during periods of arousal she was at times unable to eat or drink, and this had also happened recently. Everyone had hoped, however, that she would soon start taking nourishment again. Finally he mentioned that the girl had died this morning."

"When I called the courthouse in Klingenberg at about three, the clerk told me that Josef Michel, the dead girl's father, had come to the office at about one o'clock and had applied for a death certificate for his daughter. He said that she had suddenly developed a very high fever and had quite unexpectedly died this morning. When he was informed that only a physician could issue such a certificate after properly having viewed the body, he said that there was a physician at his home right now. The clerk called his home and spoke to Dr. Roth. Whether this person was indeed a physician is not known. Dr. Roth said that he did not have the requisite forms. He did not carry out a postmortem examination."

"Burial is to be Saturday morning."

"Upon calling the general practitioner in Klingenberg, Dr. Martin Kehler, I was informed the latter had found at his postmortem that the corpse was totally emaciated and still warm. It exhibited a number of skin abrasions. He did not attest to a natural cause of death. He suggested that an autopsy be carried out."

"He also told me he had last seen the girl in good nutritional state in October 1975. Two months ago her father had called him and he asked him to come and make a house call. A little later, however, he cancelled it."

"I have asked the Institute of Forensic Medicine at the University of Wurzburg to make preparations for the autopsy."

Signed at Aschaffenburg, July 1, 1976
Stenger
District Attorney

The media gave extensive coverage to the story. The many issues surrounding this story were hotly debated inside and outside of the media. People began to come to Klingenberg to visit Anneliese's grave and pray the rosary. Father Renz gave interviews until he was asked not to speak publicly, first by the diocese, then by his superior. Some of his photographs and tapes made their way to radio and television programs.

Father Heim received a copy of part of the taped exorcism sessions from Thea Hein and played them publicly. The police came and took the tapes from him.

Father Alt comments:

> "There were articles by journalists entirely unfamiliar with the case. The anti-Church press seized on it and dubbed the whole matter "medieval." And there were those theologians who, no longer possessing the authentic belief, said: "to hell with the devil." The latter were prominently featured on television, and they wrote lengthy articles for weekly magazines. In the local press any new development always made the front page." [43]

The state attorney's office in Aschaffenburg took a year to gather its evidence. There were rumors that the state attorney did not want to prosecute the case, but the attorney's office in Bamberg had the final word on the matter. On July 13, 1977, Father Renz, Father Alt, Josef and Anna Michel were notified that they were going to be charged with negligent homicide. Charges against Bishop Josef Stangl and Father Rodewyk were dropped.

Rumors spread of a Carmelite nun who allegedly received messages relating to Anneliese. She stated that Anneliese's body should be exhumed. This would prove, if her body had not decomposed, that the story surrounding Anneliese was true. This was to be done on February 25, 1978, before the trial. The Michels applied for an exhumation permit, stating that Anneliese was buried in an inexpensive casket and her burial had been done in haste and confusion after the postmortem examination. Eventually a permit was granted. The news traveled fast. On February 25, a small group of family and supporters, the media and authorities, gathered to witness the event. Father Renz led a group including Anna and Josef, Roswitha, Barbara, Peter and Thea Hein, from the Michel home to the cemetery. Upon reaching the grave, Anneliese's coffin was dug up and moved to the mortuary. Prior to the event the Michels were told they would be able to view Anneliese's remains. When they tried to view the remains, they were turned away by the police. [44] After responding in the affirmative to whether Father Renz wanted to see Anneliese, he too was turned away. Public officials stated that Anneliese's body showed normal corruption. Much confusion and rumors have spread about this event.

Peter, Josef, Anna and Father Renz at exhumation of Anneliese's coffin.

Considerable media attention preceded the trial which was to begin on March 30, 1978. One newspaper stated that except for the Nuremberg trials, this case had generated more commentary than any other. Portions of the grueling exorcism sessions were broadcast on German television. Her death, coupled with the fact that exorcisms were still performed in this modern day and age, shocked the West German public. It seemed every priest preached about the case, but few knew the facts. According to German law, two jurors, Erich Baumler an engineer, and Josef Becker a tailor, and three judges, Elmar Bohlender, Friizsche and von Tettau would determine the fate of the accused. The defense had no input into the juror selection.

Father Renz (67) was defended by Frithjof Lipinski, and Father Alt (40) was defended by Marianne Thora. Both lawyers were appointed by the Diocese of Wurzburg. Josef (60) and Anna (57) were defended by Erich Schmidt-Leichner, a top German lawyer who had defended numerous persons in the Nazi war-crimes trials at Nuremberg.

Erich Schmidt-Leichner chats with Father Renz
during break at trial.

The impression in the media was that the accused had little moral support from the Catholic Church. Marianne Thora seemed to share this view, as at different times she tried to obtain expert opinions on various matters and found little to no cooperation. This view is supported by the contents of the Episcopal office of Wurzburg's public letter dated August 11, 1976.

The courtroom was full on March 30, 1978 for day one of the trial with over seventy reporters or journalists present. The district courtroom was presided over by a raised wooden cross on the wall. Before the formal proceedings began, Josef Michel requested that a prayer be said as this was a case of possession. Judge Bohlender responded that they were now in a court of law not a church. The defense began by making a motion to drop all charges against the accused. This motion was rejected. A further motion to declare Professor Hans Sattes, the court appointed expert as prejudiced was also rejected.

The court was to decide what caused the death of Anneliese Michel and who was responsible.

Father Alt continues his commentary:

> "I was the first to testify on the same day. We had agreed among ourselves that this is how we would do it, because I was younger than Father Renz and better able to withstand the stress. Anneliese's parents did not testify on their own behalf. I was completely calm, I had prayed, and I had said: "Lord, this is your affair, not mine. Please guide me.""
>
> "The questioning went on for four hours that evening. For two hours I spoke without interruption."
>
> "In his introductory remarks the judge said that this was a matter of two civilians facing the court, not two servants of the Church. (Throughout the courtroom proceedings Father Renz and Father Alt were addressed as Mr. Renz and Mr. Alt) What was involved, he said, was that some citizens violated the law; it was neglect in the sense of the law. It was therefore very important to state clearly that this was not an attack against the faith, against exorcism. The only point to consider, he maintained, was the fact that the girl had starved to death. But then he wanted to know everything about exorcism, and I had the feeling I was being exhibited to the public."
>
> "I also felt I was being ridiculed by questions such as: "I assume, Father, you are not married, are you?" And everybody would laugh."
>
> "During the interrogation I said various things that he seemed to find unpalatable. For instance, I said, verbatim: "Your Honor, you may laugh about this, and even fifty million people may laugh about this, if I now tell you that we did cast out six demons. I stand by what I am saying, because I am here representing also the authentic belief of the Catholic Church." He did some swallowing on that, the people in the courtroom sat up, and the next morning it said in the papers: Even if fifty million laugh…"
>
> "When he confronted me with the assertion, that to be sure, modern theologians most certainly no longer believed in the devil, I told him this was not to be considered simply my personal faith, that it was not my responsibility either. I knew what was written in the Holy Scriptures, which I was thoroughly familiar with, and I referred him to the statements of Pope Paul VI concerning the devil." [45]

Father Alt stated to the court: "I stand by what I say because I am also representing the authentic belief of the Catholic Church."

Although these words may sound pretentious, they simply state the truth. The interesting thing is that he did nothing other than speak the true faith of the Church in front of the silence of the Bishops. These two priests must have gone through some very difficult moments, realizing that they were completely alone. The Church,

Father Alt, Father Renz, Anna and Josef
Michel during trial.

their Mother, did not defend them. This isolation may have been worse than any sentence.

Father Alt stated that he never thought Anneliese was seriously ill. He was her spiritual director until 1975. He said that Anneliese viewed her suffering as penance for priests, for the German youth, and for a certain unnamed person. She wanted the tapes made public so that people would believe there was a devil and a spiritual world. If this had been a physical illness, he and Father Renz would have sought medical help. He spoke of the various demons whom they recognized by their varying tones and expressions. The words were always in Anneliese's dialect, contrary to some reports on this point. [46] The reason Anneliese did not eat, was due to the influence the demons had on her. It is not uncommon for a possessed person to be prevented from eating by the influence of demons. There are, and have been, cases similar to Anneliese in this regard, in which the person wants to eat but the demon induces one to feel nauseous and vomit. In other cases, they may not feel nauseous but simply have an irrepressible impulse to vomit. Normally this state does not last for a long period.

On April 5, the physicians who treated Anneliese began their testimony.
Father Alt:

> Dr. Luthy came in, very handsome, graying at the temples, six feet tall. But when he started testifying in his clipped "high German," he oddly deviated from the form set by the other physicians, who had been objective, calm. In response to the question, "Did you say that if Anneliese saw Fratzen she should consult a Jesuit?" he answered with obvious agitation, very stridently, "No I have never said that," so that everybody who heard him had to think to himself, "Well, now, something obviously happened there that was not quite kosher." Anneliese's parents afterwards shook their heads. "We must say, we have never experienced anything like that." "The man did say it,"

Anna added. "I was there, I heard it myself when he said, you will have to go to a Jesuit." And of course, they would remember, because that was when they finally realized what was going on. [47]

It is interesting he suggested a Jesuit. Although the Jesuits were no more trained in this field than other orders, by chance a Jesuit was the exorcist in the famous case in Loudon France in the seventeenth century and in Washington DC in 1949 on which the movie The Exorcist is based.

Dr. Roth, who the defendants hoped would help their cause, was summoned to the stand three times. He never seemed to remember anything for certain when questioned. Father Alt had known Dr. Roth quite well. After witnessing the exorcism of May 30, 1976, Dr. Roth allegedly said "there is no injection against the devil!"

According to Father Alt, Dr. Roth made several statements inside and outside of court that simply were not true. Proceedings were initiated against Dr. Roth for perjury but the charges were dismissed.

Peter, Roswitha, Gertraud and Anneliese's friends testified next. Roswitha was asked why a physician wasn't called to attend to Anneliese. Her response was "What would you call a physician for. Possession is not like a broken leg you know". Peter and Thea Hein confirmed that Anneliese did not want to see any more physicians and that she was afraid of being diagnosed as insane and sent to the state mental institution in Lohr. On one occasion, one of Anneliese's sisters left the courtroom in tears.

Father Alt:

> It was a pleasure to listen to them, Peter and Anneliese's two sisters testified in a manner admired by everyone present. They were neatly dressed, had a fresh, engaging manner, and never got tangled in any kind of contradiction on which they could have been attacked. Anneliese's girlfriends also testified in the same style. They said what a nice person she was, what conversations they had with her, how interaction was with her. They had seen how she was sometimes sick and looked ill, and how she spent time in bed, but said that Roswitha had told them that she had been sick that way before, and it would pass. [48]

On April 5, Judge Bohlender ordered that the letters written by Fathers Renz and Alt be read in court. The defense protested. Although the state attorney agreed to the defenses request, Judge Bohlender insisted.

Father Alt:

> Bishop Josef had given the letters to the state attorney's office under the seal of strictest secrecy because he wanted to be sure that it was understood that no one had thought that the girl could die, and so forth. Now they were actually going to read them in open court. When they started I jumped up and said, very loudly, and excitedly, "I feel myself exposed by the readings of these letters, as a servant of the Church and as a priest. I am appealing to our constitution that these things not be

made public. And I am reminding you of the concordant." But they did it anyway. [49]

The court next heard excerpts of the exorcism tapes presented by Father Renz. These were to show how the prayers, within the terms of the Roman Ritual, stimulated various responses from Anneliese which indicated that she was possessed. Father Rodewyk testified that, in the extensive data he had on exorcisms, no one ever died as a result of the exorcisms. This statement by Father Rodewyk could be made by all exorcists, as there is no evidence of anyone ever dying because of exorcism prayers. There have been cases where people have died in false exorcisms. These cases have more to do with personal fanaticism or with magic rather than the ecclesiastical rite.

Father Rodewyk stated that exorcism was a prayer not a magic formula. He was absolutely convinced that Anneliese was possessed and explained she was without a will while the state lasted and was entirely normal when the state was not present.

Professor Sattes's testimony began on Monday April 10, 1978. He was a psychiatrist at the Neurological Clinic and the Polyclinic at the University of Wurzburg. Although Anneliese was treated there, he had never met her. The documents he submitted were to answer the question, whether Anneliese could have survived, had she been given medical treatment.

Professor Sattes was asked to comment on the following questions:

1. Did Anneliese suffer from a mental illness and if so, which one?
2. Could her death have been prevented by consulting a physician, possibly coupled with force feeding, either in June 1976 or at what time?
3. Could her relatives or other persons who had seen her shortly before her death have recognized her precarious condition and progressive physical deterioration?
4. Was there any indication on the tapes that she was counseled to reduce her intake of food and drink, or that she was given instructions that might have caused her death and, if so, when and by whom?

In Professor Sattes summary of Anneliese's life and medical history, Dr. Goodman noted two purported errors. First, he stated that Anneliese suffered two seizures in 1969. According to Dr. Goodman, she had one in September 1968, one on August 24, 1969, [50] and a third on June 3, 1970. [51] Secondly, Professor Sattes used an earlier statement of Dr. Luthy that showed Anneliese on Dilantin in August 1969. This file contained a retraction in this regard. After checking his records, Dr. Luthy stated that Dilantin was first prescribed in September 1972. Even if Dr. Luthy put Anneliese on Dilantin in 1969, she appeared to have had a seizure on June 3, 1970. If, as Dr. Goodman asserts, Dilantin was first given on September 5, 1972, Anneliese had been free of seizures for about 24 months. Anneliese had a seizure in June 1972. Professor Sattes also gave the impression that Tegretol was only taken until the summer of 1975, whereas there is contradictory evidence to show that she took it up until a few months before her death. Based on these two assumptions, Professor Sattes stated that the Dilantin medication successfully suppressed the seizures. This supposed suppression of the seizures due to the Dilantin then resulted in the disease seeking another outlet, turning it into a "psychogenic psychosis." To support this hypothesis, Professor Sattes referred to Dr. Luthy having suspected a paranoid psychosis in September 1973. Dr. Goodman argued that there was no evidence of Dr. Luthy stating that at that time. His summary admitted that there was no evidence anyone encouraged Anneliese to fast.

With regard to the tapes, Professor Sattes spoke of their monotony and Anneliese's unnatural speech. He saw an assumed psychogenic posture, where Anneliese assumed the role of a person dominated by one or the other demon.

During the evaluation of the case, the error that the seizures were suppressed since 1969 was repeated. It was also stated that repeated EEGs indicated damage in the left temporal region, when in truth there were only two EEGs that showed any evidence of such supposed damage. The first five EEGs showed no irregularities. That Anneliese suffered from epilepsy was considered as fact. This was important to convince the court because those who suffer epilepsy often exhibit exaggerated, and in themselves pathological, religious attitudes, and with an epileptic, even if there are no more severe seizures, there may be depressions as well as delusional periods.

Professor Sattes believed Anneliese suffered from delusional ideas about being sinful and from hallucinations involving the devil. This he said was common in religious people who suffer from depression. Her inability to go to church was another psychotic condition. Anneliese must have been sick as early as 1973. She treated conceptualizations as reality. But in early April 1976, she lost control. (It should be noted that Anneliese finished her thesis on May 28, 1976 with the last third of it being dictated to Peter and her sisters in May. Also, on April 14, 1976 Anneliese met with Dr. Veth to discuss her thesis. Later in a written statement to the court Dr. Veth referred to this meeting wherein he stated that from a physical and psychological perspective Anneliese seemed perfectly normal). Sick conceptualizations became delusional ones, so that now a severe psychotic disease, called psychogenic psychosis was produced by Anneliese by autosuggestion. The exorcism confirmed her psychotic attitudes and made things worse. Before April, the priests could have saved her by convincing her to eat. By June it was too late.

Professor Sattes concluded that since 1969, Dr. Luthy's medication suppressed the epileptic seizures. The epilepsy evolved into a psychosis, namely into seeing those demonic faces, and helped by the exorcisms, became a mental illness, being the possession. Some problems with this were, according to Dr. Goodman, that the seizures stopped before the Dilantin arrived on the scene and the faces appeared earlier, perhaps around July 1970, long before the Dilantin, assuming the September 5, 1972 date is correct.

Finally, in Professor Sattes's opinion, Anneliese would still be alive had the exorcisms not been performed. The accused should have realized that Anneliese needed help. Father Alt stated:

> Professor Sattes let it be known that he was not going to talk about religion. But given the facts of the case, he could not avoid the subject. It was his opinion that what the defendants held as belief definitely was beyond normal psychological and

religious conceptualization.

Judge Bohlender then requested that Professor Sattes pay close attention to us, because it might be possible that, due to lack of mental competency, he may not be able to sentence us. He mentioned some legal provision-paragraph 20 or 21, I believe. The man would you believe it, actually made an effort to observe us. [52]

When asked in cross examination what he would have done, Professor Sattes stated that he would have tranquilized Anneliese, force fed her and treated her with electric shock.

Marianne Thora felt it might be helpful to provide their own experts to formulate a psychiatric evaluation of their clients. She had a hard time finding anyone, as no one wanted to get involved. This is often the case. There are psychiatrists who in private acknowledge that demons exist and exorcism can provide positive results, but to admit this publicly is another thing. In general, psychiatrists speak publicly against possession, and psychiatrists who are open to the possibility of possession usually do not speak publicly in this regard. In this case it appears there were no believing psychiatrists who wanted to become involved. Marianne Thora finally found two doctors from the University of Ulm. Dr. Alfred Lungerhausen was chairman of the Psychiatry department and was director of the university hospital at Gunzburg and Dr. Gerd Klaus Kohler was the medical superintendent of a psychiatric clinic in Duisburg.

The two psychiatrists submitted a long (103 pages) and complex paper which included the results of their examination of Father Alt and Father Renz. With regard to Father Renz, they found his movements and facial expressions "pastoral," betraying his lifelong priestly activity. They found his answers rambling but "definite and precise." They found it curious that he was incapable of critical evaluation concerning the topic of exorcism, when his intellectual abilities in other areas were normal. There was no indication of schizophrenia, manic depression, psychosis etc. He was a "deeply religious personality rooted in magico-mystical thinking." They seemed to support Professor Sattes's hypothesis. They noted that Dr. Luthy did not prescribe Dilantin until September 1972, but agreed that the Dilantin suppressed the seizures. They said Anneliese underwent a serious paranoid psychotic episode in 1973. In 1975, she developed the delusion of possession. It was a psychogenic psychosis. The two priests offered content and form for Anneliese's psychotic behavior. Also they believed the two priests showed a readiness to accept what Anneliese offered them. Anneliese's psychosis had its beginning in childhood. She had a disturbed sexual development. She identified with her authoritarian father's superego while suppressing her own feelings of hatred, thus making her aggressive.

Today, psychoanalysis has been discredited among many psychiatric professionals. It has been shown that many psychoanalytic evaluations have been more fantasy or the creativity of the specialist than fact or reality.

The two psychiatrists believed the priests had acted out of religious conviction. This conviction came "from naive, needless to say primitive religious views. Both of them leaned toward magico-mystical ideas that were, to say the least, unusual for theologians of our time." Anneliese's demons were the expression of a naive piety. The exorcisms made things worse. Their diagnosis, for the most part, was as per Professor Sattes. Anneliese's personality was determined by her epilepsy. This developed into a schizophrenic-like psychosis or psychogenic psychosis with depressive and delusional disturbances.

Father Alt comments on one aspect of Dr. Kohler's remarks:

> Dr. Kohler spoke of Tegretol, (saying) that it could, with long-term application, produce what he called a "shifting of the field," and for that reason it was a dangerous drug, but the court did not pick up on that. Dr. Lungershausen admitted the possibility there were religious matters that psychology had no key to. In every other respect, both went along completely with the theories of Professor Sattes.
>
> Frau Thora was very disappointed. She thought these two psychiatrists would speak in our favor. We had talked extensively with them. During a pause I went up to Dr. Lungershausen and said, "Dr. Lungershausen, you are thoroughly familiar with my case. Please tell me: How do you explain the condition in which I found myself during that night, when I was so severely beset by something? How do you explain that all of a sudden there was a fragrance of violets and everything was over? After all, I had been completely calm; I did not even know Anneliese at the time; I had only heard of her." He answered, "Well, that is something known from statistics," and when I asked him to tell me what he meant, he just smiled, as if to say: How could anything be explained to a simple priest?" [53]

The prosecution asked that all four accused be found guilty of negligent homicide due to their failure to act. They asked only that the priests be fined and that no punishment be rendered to the parents as the loss of their daughter had been enough punishment.

Marianne Thora demanded that the defendants be acquitted. Anneliese had refused any further medical help as she believed it was no help to her and she put her life in God's hands. This, she thought, was her moral and constitutional right.

When Judge Bohlender read the courts verdict on April 21, 1978, the medical expert's opinions provided by the prosecution had been accepted in its entirety. Those involved could not have known the epilepsy had evolved into a psychosis. In May 1976, at the latest, Anneliese no longer had the ability to determine and deal with her own well-being. The exorcism sessions aggravated her condition. The defendants should have sought medical help. The court said, had Anneliese been given medical treatment, perhaps force fed even a week before her death her life could have been saved. The sentence therefore states that medical attention must have been sought even though they were convinced the problem was spiritual. This means that any doctor, psychiatrist or perhaps state employee who considered that an exorcism is injurious to one's health may legally intervene and take over such a case.

One of Anneliese's sister's testified that Anneliese made it clear that she did not want to be sent to a mental institution where she would be sedated and force fed.

All four defendants were sentenced to six months in prison, which was suspended, with three years' probation. Father Alt was fined 4800 deutschmarks, and Father Renz 3600 deutschmarks. They were also responsible for court costs. The four accused initially appealed the court's decision. After reflecting on the whole process, partly due to financial reasons and partly due to the fact that all involved had no confidence that a fair court decision could be reached, they decided to withdraw their appeal. It should be noted that the court costs for the priests were incurred by the Diocese of Wurzburg. Had the courts' decision been appealed, the priests would have been responsible for any additional legal costs. All the files relating to this court case and the diocesan files related to this story are not presently available to the public.

One should not be shocked by the fact the court came to the verdict it did or that the public had such distain for the defendants. Where judgments are made by the courts on controversial matters the defendants are often supported by the public. Here the parents and the two accused priests were under terrible pressure, as the Law, the Church, the media, and public opinion were for the most part all against them.

Chapter IX

LIFE GOES ON

Anneliese, her family, Peter, the Heins, the priests and their Bishop, all believed that medical and psychological remedies had proven unsuccessful. They also believed Anneliese's condition ultimately met the criteria of possession. After much time, consultation and several requests to the Bishop, permission was granted to begin the exorcism prayers. In a modern world where religious beliefs have become marginalized, where within the Catholic Church many of its long held truths have come under attack from inside and outside its doors, there should be little doubt that the opinions of what really happened to Anneliese Michel would be divided. For those who do not believe in God, demons do not exist, and this makes exorcism an event for medieval history. Although a detailed psychiatric evaluation of Anneliese was never performed, epilepsy and psychological illness were plausible causes for a person suffering some of the symptoms Anneliese exhibited. There were however, many things that could not be explained by this diagnosis. For those who believe in God and the New Testament, possession is a plausible cause for Anneliese's suffering. It is clear that Anneliese, those close to her and several priests familiar with her case, all believed she suffered from possession, that her faith in God and the Catholic Church was not in question, and more importantly, she suffered tremendously and offered these sufferings up to her Savior.

Shortly after Anneliese's death, various rumours circulated, and the public was looking to the Bishop's office for clarification. The following letter dated August 11, 1976 was intended to address these concerns:

Wurzburg August 11, 1976

Clarification on the Events in Klingenberg

The death of the university student Anneliese Michel in Klingenberg on July 1, 1976 has brought many questions before the public, questions that are directed, not least of all, to the Bishop of Wurzburg and to the Episcopal authorities of Wurzburg. The public expects answers which do nothing to hush the matter up, but which seek, as far as possible, to bring clarity to this tragic event. What follows then is the position taken by the Bishop and the Episcopal Office of Wurzburg.

What does the church teach about the devil and demons?

The New Testament tells us that Jesus expelled demons. One finds in some pronouncements of the Church (e.g. of the Fourth Lateran Council of 1215) statements about the devil. There applies to these statements what must be taken into consideration with all human teachings: It is to be understood within the background of the times in which they were given and in the proper context.

> 1. A glance at the world view of the Bible shows us that people from that culture could not imagine a world without demons. In addition to other influences, one may point out the contribution of our immediate experience, that evil often assails mankind as if it were an inescapable power, that mankind not seldom feels in himself an urge towards evil. This world view is also presupposed in the later corresponding ecclesiastical statements, without this world view having to be regarded in particulars as a binding part of Church teaching.
> 2. When one takes into consideration the context in which such statements occur then it becomes apparent that where there is talk of the devil or demons, in the final analysis, we are dealing with the power of God. Both the Bible and ecclesiastical pronouncements do not then wish to set forth a teaching about the Evil One, a "Satanology". The real point of their teachings is to say that God and only God is stronger than all evil.
> 3. Statements about evil or the devil are therefore false and contradict the spirit of the New Testament and the ecclesiastical tradition

-where they claim to be able to differentiate something about the nature and behavior of the devil or demons;

-where they intend to be a threatening message [Drohbotscaft], to frighten people rather than to arouse trust in God who can have no serious rival in this world.

What does the Church understand by "possession" and "exorcism"?

The idea of "possession" has played a disastrous role in the history of the Church, above all in the Middle Ages. This was, at the time, only possible-apart from other cultural and historical reasons-because fundamental truths of the Christian faith were neglected.

> 1. The Church teaches that mankind enjoys the salvation of God by faith and baptism and that those who are not baptized also participate in the salvation of God. So mankind is fundamentally withdrawn from the power of [the] evil [one]. It therefore contradicts the express faith of the Church to maintain that someone was already "cursed in his mother's womb" or that "the evil spirits are stronger than the good".
> 2. What is described as "possession" can, according to present day views, include two conditions: It can be – and this is mostly the case – a serious sickness. It can also be – such experiences of the mystics hardly permit us to deny it – a particularly deep emersion of someone in the Passion of Jesus, which according to the Bible went to the point of the experience of feeling abandoned by God. Examples of this are known from the lives of the saints.

3. Hence, by "exorcism" one is not to understand the driving out of the devil by magical means. Exorcism is nothing other than the prayer of the Church in the name of Jesus for someone who no longer has command of himself, who feels himself abandoned, who can himself no longer pray. Anyone who understands exorcism differently or carries it out otherwise, is opposed to the Church's understanding of the faith.

4. This prayer, of course, in no way excludes medical aid, indeed it requires it. Prayer, according to the Christian understanding, does not mean to compel God to do something, but rather to conform oneself to the will of God. But God desires we help each other with all the means available. For the sick these means include medical help. To pray for someone withholding medical treatment is unchristian.

5. How should one judge the occurrences in Klingenberg?

   1. At the moment a definitive judgment on the Klingenberg occurrences is not possible, since the facts of the case are not completely known by the Office of the Bishop. The knowledge of the doctors who treated Anneliese is not presently available since they are bound by their professional secrecy. The testimony of specialists is not yet at hand. The symptoms that have shown themselves – so far as they are known – are not foreign to psychiatrists. They belong to the realm of medicine. Moreover, the Roman Ritual describes as unworthy of belief statements in which the "demon" identifies himself with those who are dead (Tit.XXII, Cap.I.n. 14).

   2. The Bishop granted the permission to pray the exorcism in the conviction that he ought not to deny to the young girl, her family and the priests their petition for what was seen as their last hope and was awaited with great confidence. What was decisive for the Bishop was that Anneliese Michel with great readiness took upon herself the hard trial of her suffering as a religious person, participating in the cross of Christ, wherein she naturally expected the help of the Church.

   3. The public distribution of the recordings, which contain the statements of the patient, constitutes a regrettable attack on privacy. One of the commissioned priests who has been involved in this damages his duty to maintain silence and acts contrary to the directives of the Roman Ritual which indicates that for the person affected by the exorcism is to be prayed "aside from the crowd' and with only a "few" present; the purpose of this being to protect the personal rights of the party involved.

   4. An exorcism can never substitute for medical help. Those statements should be decisively rejected in which the impression could be given that treatment in a psychiatric hospital is some kind of evil from which a patient must be protected.

   5. A criminal investigation of the matter is a matter for the authorities of the State.

What consequences does the Episcopal authority plan to draw from these occurrences?

In the view of the Episcopal Authorities consequences touching on ecclesiastic discipline and of a theological-scientific and pastoral nature must be drawn.

   1. The diocesan authorities reserve to themselves-independently of a judicial inquiry-inner ecclesiastical proceedings on account of possible breaches of duty. In these proceedings criminal facts will not be dealt with, rather questions of Church

teaching and pastoral discipline.

2. The diocesan authorities request that professional theologians, and also representatives of other relevant scientific disciplines, such as psychology, psychiatry, sociology, et al., as far as possible in an interdisciplinary investigation, further clarify the questions which surround such occurrences.

3. The diocesan authorities will take the necessary steps for the care of souls, the work of proclamation and formation and-while also watching over many other areas-make available aids in order to check disastrous forms of so-called piety and to smooth the way for an understanding of the faith as is needed for the difficulties of our times. It cannot be task of the Church to frighten people about evil. Whoever behaves in that way, acts irresponsibly. The task of the Church is to give people trust and assurance from faith about salvation, to show them the meaning of their lives and sufferings and to enable them to withstand evil and pursue the good.

Wurzburg, August 11, 1976

+ Josef
Bishop of Wurzburg

The statement pertaining to an attack on one's privacy relating to the public distribution of the tapes is not applicable here. Anneliese was in favour of disclosing the words of the demons because, as a fervent Christian, she wanted the world to believe in the spiritual realm. She was consoled by the fact that her pain and suffering would be for the good of others. Her parents also shared this view.

It is true that the Roman Ritual cautions exorcists when a demon claims to be a human soul. Today however, this advice is debated by many exorcists. The new version of the Rite of Exorcisms (1999) does not contain this advice.

"The chancery of the Bishopric of Wurzburg did not manage the case of possession in the face of the public well. Inside the chancery there were differing opinions. Bishop Dr. Stangl was convinced of the authenticity of the case. Nevertheless, there appeared on the 11 of August 1976 the afore stated Episcopal clarification. Contrary to the clear doctrine of the Church, which had been taught for the last 2000 years, the Bishop of Wurzburg explained that there was no devil and that possession is a sickness or a particular kind of participation in the sufferings of Christ. Till this day this shameful document has never been revoked." [54]

How does one view Bishop Stangl's position, from granting permission to perform the exorcism sessions with prayerful and heartfelt support to denying the existence of the devil only weeks after Anneliese's death? One can only speculate as to the reason. Did he come to the realization that a mistake had been made, or was he simply under pressure from his fellow Bishops and his own chancery to minimize the negative impact the Church was subjected to as a result of this case?

Bishop Josef Stangl stated that in the future he would only approve an exorcism if the possessed person agreed to the presence of a physician during the ritual. This was a dangerous precedent. It put at risk the possibility of the Church and its experts in spiritual and religious matters being subject to science, and doctors who may not believe in such matters.

It is interesting to note that Bishop Joseph Stangl consecrated Father Joseph Ratzinger (Benedict XVI) a Bishop in Munich on May 28, 1977. Bishop Stangl suffered much from this event. He resigned on January 8, 1979 and soon after suffered a stroke that his friends said was brought on by the grief the case caused him. He died on April 8, 1979. On April 11, Joseph Ratzinger (then archbishop of Munich) was among the clergy concelebrating the funeral mass for Bishop Stangl. He was remembered as a pious, good natured and friendly man. From a deep faith, he firmly believed that permission to pray the exorcism prayers for Anneliese Michel would be able to help her. His last years were overshadowed by negative media that misunderstood him and the Klingenberg Case.

Joseph Cardinal Hoffner, head of the German Bishops Conference, publicly confirmed on April 28, 1978 that there is a fundamental possibility of demonic possession as it pertained to the Klingenberg Case.

With regard to the judge in this case, one can only wonder if he erred when he questioned the religious beliefs of the accused. Judge Bohlender commented that the priest's beliefs with regard to the devil were not in tune with modern theologians. This issue should not have affected the verdict either way.

An interdisciplinary commission comprised of theologians, psychiatrists, psychologists etc., was appointed by the German Conference of Bishops to address various matters including possession, exorcism and the Klingenberg case. The commission members included Cardinal Joseph Hoffner (Archbishop of Cologne), Walter Kasper (university professor of theology), Bishop of Rottenburg-Stuttgart (1987) and Cardinal (February 21, 2001), Karl Lehmann University professor of theology, Bishop of Mainz (1983) and Cardinal (January 28, 2001), Dr. Emile Joseph Lengeling (university professor and liturgical expert at University of Munster), Dr. P. Ulrich Niemann S. J. (university professor of psychoanalysis), and Dr. Johannes Mischo (teaching professor of parapsychology at the University of Frieburg). A paper written by Mischo and Niemann in 1983 included their belief that Anneliese had suffered from mental illness. In 1984, the commission petitioned Rome to change the exorcism rite. One concern was the practice of speaking directly to the demon, which they believed caused damage by confirming and reinforcing the patient's belief that they were possessed.

Father Alt in his commentary thirty years later stated the following:

> "Investigations were undertaken that do not deserve the name. Some individuals with important names thought they were able to pass judgment on us. They knew none of those who took part, neither Father Arnold Renz, the parents, the sisters of Anneliese, nor myself. There were no telephone calls, no exchange of letters, no statements made on our part. But there was a condemnation, a so-called judgment with an official stamp of approval. They knew it all. This was all written down and made public as an interdisciplinary investigation commissioned by the German Bishop's Conference." [55]

During a BBC interview dated April 10, 1978, Peter addressed several issues with the interviewer. With regard to the exorcism sessions, Peter stated, "We asked specialists in exorcism to come and to ascertain if Anneliese was really possessed. They evaluated her, we described what had happened. They believed that she was possessed." Peter described the last time he saw Anneliese alive on June 30, 1976: "She was terribly thin, her eyes were black, she was bruised, but as I always said, she had strength in her." Peter was asked, "Do you yourself really believe that Anneliese was possessed?" He responded, "Yes I believe it." Interviewer, "Most people upon hearing the story of Anneliese Michel, believe she suffered from delusion and mental illness and the exorcism should have been stopped and a doctor forced upon her." Peter responded, "I still believe she was possessed, still now. Also I think no doctor could have helped her. She told me that she could help other people through her sufferings."

After the death of Anneliese, Anna Michel stated: "The worst of the matter is, not that so much has been written about this case, but that in spite of it all, no one believes in the devil."

In an article printed on November 11, 2005 by Elizabeth Day for the Telegraph, Anna Michel was quoted as follows: "I don't want to see the film *The Exorcism of Emily Rose* and I don't know anything about it. I miss Anneliese, of course. She was my daughter. I can see her grave from the house. I visit it often, taking flowers. I know that we did the right thing because I saw the sign of Christ in her hands. She died to save lost souls, to atone for their sins. Anneliese was a kind, loving, sweet and obedient girl. But when she was possessed, it was something unnatural, something that you cannot explain."

The Michels suffered financially as a result of the trial's outcome. Some of the people in their community lobbied to have the family leave Klingenberg. Father Arnold Renz died on May 17, 1986.

Josef Michel died in 1989.

Father Ernst Alt was granted a private audience in Rome with Pope John Paul II in 1996.

Peter subsequently married Maria Klug. He is a school teacher and lives with Maria and their six children in Germany. Although he does not speak publicly about this story, he believes as he did at the time, that Anneliese suffered from possession. His relationship and experiences with Anneliese strengthened his Catholic faith.[56]

Anna and Roswitha live in Klingenberg. Roswitha, while supporting the family's belief in Anneliese's suffering of possession at the time, later believed that Anneliese's sufferings may have had a psychological explanation.

Peter and Thea Hein considered themselves fortunate that they were not part of the accused at the trial. They were absent from the events surrounding Anneliese during the last month of her life because Peter was suffering from meningitis and was in the hospital. Peter is a retired master varnisher and resides in Leidersbach, Germany. Thea died on August 12, 2008 after suffering several strokes.

Anna Michel died on June 19, 2012 at the age of 92.

Father Ernst Alt is retired and lives in southern Germany.

CONCLUSION

Anneliese Michel, the person, is too often lost in the events of this story, the subjects of possession/exorcism and mental illness, the media attention and her tragic death. Those who knew Anneliese described her as intelligent, reserved in manner and speech, sensitive, kind, polite and deeply religious. She had a beautiful smile. She was very knowledgeable of the Catholic faith, which she quietly and faithfully put into practice. She led an active prayer and sacramental life. With a clear understanding of the role of suffering from a Christian perspective, she accepted her trials and tribulations in life. Outside the events which caused her varying degrees of suffering, she led a normal and happy life pursuing all the normal things many young ladies do. She fell in love with a fellow classmate whom she planned to marry in the fall of 1976 and thus fulfill her dream of becoming a school teacher and have a family.

Considering the field of mental pathologies and acknowledging the existence of the spiritual world, when we became familiar with the circumstances surrounding this case, the authors were able to state beyond a reasonable doubt that Anneliese did not suffer from mental illness. What we see in her behavior comes not from a state of mental illness, but from the demonic possession she was suffering. The depression she endured was the normal consequence of the situation in which she lived. During the last part of her life, she suffered from a compulsion which was caused by the influence of the demons on her mind. This was manifested through the repetition of pious acts such as genuflections and prayers. This was part of the cross which God permitted.

Anneliese suffered physically, mentally and spiritually. She suffered the physical effects of seizure or seizure-like symptoms, brief periods of unconsciousness, and the inability at times to eat, sleep, walk and speak. There were depression-like symptoms which became constant. At times her spiritual desires to pray, go to confession, go to mass and receive Holy Communion were interfered with or not permitted. She suffered because no one seemed able to help her situation, except through prayer, which gave her varying degrees of relief. She suffered the dread of demonic faces and other associated afflictions that she experienced in this regard. Drawing on her faith, she accepted these sufferings and offered them to God in expiation for the sins of others. She continued to live her life in a heroic manner despite these formidable challenges. Apart from these afflictions, she appeared to live and function as a happy, normal person.

In the midst of these sufferings, her family and priests believed Anneliese received divine consolations in the form of locutions and that she felt the presence of Jesus, Mary, various saints, and several deceased relatives. Anneliese subsequently received visions of Jesus and Mary, such as the one described by Anna Michel and Thea Hein in which Mary appeared to her and asked if she was willing to offer her sufferings to God.

Anneliese, her family, Peter, the Heins, Father Renz, Father Alt, Father Rodewyk, Bishop Stangl, and several other priests who were familiar with this case, believed that Anneliese suffered from possession. As a result, the only remedy to alleviate Anneliese's condition was to pray the prayers of exorcism. They believed the exorcism prayers would eventually be successful and Anneliese would be liberated. If the exorcism had been successful, perhaps only the family, friends and priests would have come to know of the events pertaining to Anneliese's life.

Anneliese seems to have come to the conclusion in April or May 1976 that her offering may include giving up her life. When asked why they would not leave, the demons repeatedly responded that they were not permitted to do so. Since Anneliese offered her sufferings to God and died on July 1, 1976, as she foretold as being the date of the resolution to her condition, one may speculate that God permitted this to happen.

Since these events may be regarded from a spiritual perspective as a way of participating in Christ's sufferings, the death of Anneliese was by no means a failure of exorcism. It has to be understood in the same way as Christ's death. What may be seen, in the eyes of the world, as a failure, may actually be success in the eyes of God. Anneliese did everything she could to extricate the tyranny of the demons, and the priests did everything they could to free her of them. So why would God permit her to die? As an expiatory sacrifice?

The idea that sufferings offered with love, resignation and patience have salvific value, is central to Christian Theology. These sufferings become graces for the salvation of others. The sacrifice on the Cross two thousand years ago cannot be understood without this concept of expiation. In this new German version of Calvary everyone did what they thought was best, but God accepted the sacrifice permitting Anneliese's death.

God permitted the demons to stop Anneliese from eating in the same way as throughout history He allowed executioners to accomplish the martyrdom of their victims, even though they prayed and asked for their liberation from their captives.

The Michels and the two priests suffered tremendously following Anneliese's death and the verdict of the court. In some ways, they suffered for the rest of their lives with the terrible burden of being surrounded by people who considered them guilty in spite of knowing in good conscience they did the best they could for Anneliese. This sentence was for life.

This whole affair had another consequence. It effectively stopped exorcisms in

Germany. Although exorcisms were not a common occurrence in Germany at the time, after this bitter event it seemed that no Bishop wanted to have anything to do with the power to dismiss demons, which was granted by Jesus to His Apostles. Rarely had such an event affected the Church so adversely in one country.

Was the judge's verdict correct in this case?

The one aspect of this story in which the authors do not share the same opinion on, is the verdict of the court. As there is a clear discrepancy between the authors, the book continues with two separate conclusions.

The following are Father Fortea's thoughts on the court's verdict:

> I believe in spite of the fact that the parents and priests acted in good faith with Anneliese's best interests in mind, when Anneliese's health was in danger, medical attention should have been sought. In this case, the parents and priests believed that Anneliese's condition could only be solved through prayer. I would add: Josef and Anna Michel and Father Renz and Father Alt were people of integrity and did their best according to their consciences.
>
> In spite of the foregoing, Anneliese should have been admitted to a hospital when her condition became serious. I recognize that those close to her at the time were not aware of the threat of death, as they were dealing with a situation in which the guidelines to be followed were not written anywhere.
>
> Reflecting on this story, natural reason dictates that Anneliese should have been taken to a hospital. Failure to do so was an error made in good faith, without desire to harm and with only Anneliese's welfare in mind. Nevertheless, it was an error under the guidelines of exorcism and under the law. The judge was required to give a verdict according to the objective facts. There was negligence under the law. No other verdict could have been given. The judge had no alternative. Render unto Caesar what is Caesar's.
>
> Clearly, there are two perspectives to be addressed. Priests have a duty to expel the demons from a possessed person, whereas a judge has a duty to rule on whether there was a breach of the law as it pertains to protecting the physical well-being of a person. Had the judge rendered a verdict of innocence in this case, it would in effect state that those who incur responsibility for another person's physical well-being and who do not act according to the law, can justify any culpable actions based on religious beliefs.
>
> Perhaps a fictitious example may shed some light on this. An abbot in a monastery is aware that one of his monks refused to eat after he claimed to have received a divine message, and the monk states he will not die if he does not eat. What should the abbot do? It would be appropriate for the abbot to wait a reasonable period of time to test the authenticity of the supposed message. After a reasonable time, if the monk's physical condition puts his life in danger, the abbot must inform the police or appropriate authorities so they can intervene to help him.
>
> As is evident in the case above of the monk fasting and in one possessed who has stopped eating, religious and legal issues form an intersection. When we speak about the spiritual well-being of a person, it is for the religious authorities to decide what course of action to take. In the case of Anneliese, the religious authorities decided to perform an exorcism. On the other hand, when the issue becomes one of the physical well-being of the person, Civil Law is applicable. The judge must

rule based on the facts of the case, not on the participant's intentions or beliefs (such as whether Anneliese suffered possession or not). The participant's beliefs and intentions must not affect the judge's verdict.

It is however, hard to find a case like this one, where spiritual and physical, religious and legal matters are so interrelated. It is a complex case involving many issues and there is much to be learned from it. Anneliese sacrificed herself and entered the Kingdom of Heaven as a martyr. Her family joined her during this long period of exorcism, suffering with her, and encouraging her during her carrying of this cross. The priests did everything in their power to release Anneliese from her possession. The decision not to seek medical attention was, in hindsight, an error in judgment. Lastly, the court rendered a fair verdict and a light sentence was issued, considering the circumstances of this case. I believe in demonic possession, I believe in the good faith of the priests, but as a judge I would have rendered the same sentence. If not, any religious leader could do anything based on freedom of belief. He could always say: my creed permits me to do so. The Law must render its verdict based on common sense. The facts are to be judged by the court, not on the beliefs or the intentions of the parties involved. In this case there was an error that led to negligence, a negligence that led to a death. The judge did what was correct.

Here ends Father Fortea's thoughts on the courts verdict.

The following are Lawrence LeBlanc's thoughts on the judge's verdict:

Had the persons responsible for deciding whether this case should go to trial been aware of all the facts and information pertaining to the events leading up to Anneliese's death and objectively evaluated these facts without undue influence of the public and the media, I do not believe this case would ever have gone to trial. Due to pressure from the media and the public, who were shocked by the story, accompanied by a general lack of knowledge of possession and exorcism, this case became a public relations nightmare for the Catholic Church and the judicial system in Germany.

As in all trials, the judge was obliged to render justice. According to the world the verdict seemed correct. However, if the spiritual world exists, the verdict may have been in error. Justice is based on the simple premise of convicting those who commit a crime, rather than convicting the innocent. In this case, the innocent were convicted. In spite of this, I believe that over time history will pass judgment in favor of the defendants. Initially many of those who became familiar with this case based their judgments or opinions on a biased media presentation of the facts of this story. The public had little or no knowledge of what the family and priests witnessed and experienced. One must ask, where were the ecclesiastics who remained silent at this time? Where were those who believed in possession/exorcism, and where were they in their defense?

The two aspects of the trial which need to be addressed are: The element of mental illness versus possession, and whether there was neglect on the part of the parents and priests.

The court set out to determine if Anneliese suffered from mental illness, and if her parents and priests could have recognized her precarious condition shortly before her death, and if her death could have been prevented.

The court's verdict was based on accepting the evidence of Anneliese being diagnosed as suffering from mental illness. If the court and psychologists were not open to the possibility of possession and exorcism being its remedy, there is really no other explanation than mental illness for Anneliese's condition. Anneliese suffered certain symptoms which were similar to epilepsy and mental illness. There were however, many things that could not be explained by mental illness that could be explained by possession.

Judge Harald Grochtmann noted that there is legal precedent where the court has acknowledged that possession exists. This was done without attempting to determine the source of the possession. In this case the court should have examined what the characteristics of possession were, then examined the facts concerning Anneliese as it pertained to characteristics of possession (understanding unknown languages, aversion to sacred objects, inability to eat, extraordinary strength, inexplicable weight, etc.) and compared these characteristics with other similar cases of possession. There are cases where possessed persons have suffered similar symptoms to Anneliese and were healed after a successful exorcism.

The court must acknowledge the facts, regardless of whether they are explicable or not. With regard to possession, the judges should have differentiated the facts and their possible consequences from the question of the source or cause of such powers and the conclusions to be drawn from them. The court did not make this distinction.

Although the court explained that possession is a religious and theological phenomenon, the fact remains that regardless of questions of faith, many people have been healed of possession by exorcism. This is what Schott, a professor of Medical history at the University of Freiburg, talked about during a television show "Spiritual Healing-What is it all about?" (ZDF, September 17, 1985). According to Schott, exorcism is also a kind of healing. Inexplicable cases of healing at Lourdes, Fatima, and other places have occurred where there is no medical or scientific explanation for them. In these cases, a court can only recognize the fact that these people were terminally ill and are now completely healthy. They are unable to address the source of the healings. However, the court can and must examine if there is a natural explanation for such phenomena. Where there is no natural explanation the court should acknowledge that there is no natural explanation. [57]

Fischer and Schiedermair, who welcomed the courts verdict in this case, state: "Indeed not only theologians, but also thoughtful Christians should be surprised at the kind of ideological claims and instructions found in the verdict of Aschaffenburg." These authors state that having confidence in such things as miracles signifies a loss of reality. They also state that it is incomprehensible that, according to section 21 of the German Penal Code, the court saw the possibility of diminished responsibility of the defendants because they believed in the personal existence of the devil. [58]

That the devil exists is not only the doctrine of the Catholic Church, but also of the Orthodox and most Protestant churches. Therefore, one cannot say that all Christians are potentially mentally ill for having such a belief.

A miraculous healing at Lourdes and a successful exorcism are similar in that they share the way in which they are healed. In opposition to medical treatment, this kind of treatment has no direct influence. Exorcism is no more than a set of prayers, the same in that at Lourdes, people pray to be cured. It is the nature of prayer that we have no influence on whether or not our prayers will be answered. So when Schott describes exorcism as a kind of healing he could not have meant that there is a direct causality between the role of the priest during the exorcism and the healing of the possessed person. He could only have meant that a person tortured by the dreadful manifestations of possession had been completely freed from them after an exorcism. The healing was real and the treatment was exorcism. [59]

In the same way as a court cannot forbid an incurably ill person to go to Lourdes hoping to be miraculously healed there, it cannot condemn prayers for a possessed person during an exorcism. In democratic states, this is guaranteed by common law. The German Republic emphasizes this responsibility in front of God and the people. Therefore, the state can only welcome prayers that help a possessed person to be freed from their torments, provided that necessary medical care is sought when or where required. [60]

In spite of multiple visits to neurologists and psychologists, a psychological evaluation was never done on Anneliese. She was told she suffered from symptoms similar to epilepsy. The statements that Anneliese was sexually underdeveloped and suffering a neurosis caused by a domineering father and a hatred for her mother were never proven by serious evidence and can be considered no more than conjecture derived from the subjective field of psychology. Moreover, there is compelling evidence to the contrary. The court did not consider seriously the possibility of possession and accepted the testimony purporting that Anneliese was mentally ill. If she was found mentally ill, the door would be opened for the court to transfer culpability for Anneliese's death to her caregivers.

From the late 1960's until mid 1975, it is well documented that Anneliese (with Anna or Peter) made multiple visits to various psychologists, neurologists and family physicians seeking the cause and remedy to her condition. Although Anneliese stated that the medication left her depressed and tired, she continued to take it until shortly before her death. In spite of the medical help and medication, her torments continued. Anneliese believed that she had exhausted all possibilities for a medical solution to her condition. She subsequently decided not to seek any further medical help. Anneliese had a deep fear of being diagnosed as mentally ill and sent to an institution. Those close to her were aware of this and respected her wishes when addressing this issue. It was her moral and legal right not to seek further medical assistance.

Several times prior to her death, Anneliese had been unable to eat and became very thin and then recovered and returned to a normal weight. This occurred in the summer of 1975, February 1976 and April 1976. Anneliese stated that she would gladly eat but was not allowed to. This is not uncommon in cases similar to Anneliese's where the person afflicted is not allowed to eat.

In May 1976, Joseph called Dr. Kelher requesting he make a house call but called back to cancel it. Dr. Kelher testified that Anneliese was in good health after seeing her in October 1975.

On May 30, 1976, Dr. Roth agreed to Father Alt's request to attend an exorcism session because Anneliese's condition had worsened. They discussed giving Anneliese something to calm her down. Dr. Roth decided not to administer any medication to Anneliese as he did not know how she would react. Dr. Roth wrote letters or certificates on two occasions to allow Anneliese to postpone the date to complete her practice teaching due to her condition.

On June 27, 1976, Joseph called Father Alt, and Father Alt suggested calling a doctor. Anneliese refused. Father Alt's last visit to Klingenberg was on June 8, 1976. The foregoing three instances clearly evidence that those close to Anneliese saw medical attention as a potential benefit for Anneliese's condition in spite of her refusal to entertain medical assistance.

On June 30, 1976, the eve of Anneliese's death, Joseph, Anna, Roswitha, Barbara, Peter and Father Renz were with Anneliese. The people present knew and loved Anneliese most, and had witnessed what she had undergone over the last days, weeks, months and years. All present came to believe Anneliese suffered from possession. All present dedicated themselves to helping Anneliese in her sufferings. All present knew Anneliese was not mentally ill. All present did not recognize that Anneliese's life was in danger. The two things most often discussed by Anneliese, Peter and her family prior to her death, were the July resolution to Anneliese's condition and whether medical assistance should have been sought. The role of Father Renz and Father Alt was to provide spiritual counseling and pray the exorcism prayers for Anneliese, which they did with dedication and perseverance. All believed Anneliese made lucid decisions and it was her moral and legal right to refuse medical attention.

There is no doubt that starvation or malnutrition was the primary cause of death. Physical exhaustion combined with her previously diagnosed circulatory problems and Tegretol, could be considered as contributing factors to her death.

In hindsight, Anneliese should have been artificially fed. But just as it is not fair to prosecute a doctor after an unsuccessful treatment that has been carried out to the doctor's best ability, it is not just to find the priests or the parents guilty of neglect because they did not exert enough influence on Anneliese to seek further medical help against her will.

Perhaps Anneliese's boyfriend Peter's comments best represent the mindset of those closest to Anneliese as it pertained to her last days: "In the end we didn't know what to do, since nothing was helping. We were really hoping in her statement; On July 1 there will come a change. Of course, that things would happen as they did we would never have imagined. It is very difficult in hindsight to say what we could have done differently. This is the case also when one is dealing with the supernatural. Should we have brought her to a mental hospital? That is something that she absolutely did not want. In that case she would have been brought to the hospital in Lohr and would have died there. Then I would have reproached myself for the rest of my life." [61]

The Klingenberg Case is complex, involving physical, spiritual, religious and legal matters from which much can be learned. Those closest to Anneliese (her parents, sisters, her boyfriend Peter and Father Renz and Father Alt) were all people of integrity who did everything they could under the circumstances. There was no moral or ethical culpability on their part, therefore there should be no culpability under the law.

One cannot fail to recognize the connection of Anneliese's sufferings, particularly during holy week of 1976, with the sufferings of Jesus Christ. Anneliese offered her sufferings to God and she died a martyr.

Although many questions remain, one can offer a few thoughts on the message or meaning of Anneliese Michel's life: God chose her for this mission before she was born. He permitted the demons to afflict her and ultimately possess her. Of her own free will Anneliese agreed to continue her sufferings and offered these sufferings to God for the benefit of others. God showed the world through Anneliese, at a time when belief in the supernatural had diminished, that hell and demons are real, that a spiritual world exists and a battle is being waged by good and evil forces for the soul of every human being.

Here ends Lawrence LeBlanc's thoughts on the courts verdict.

PART II

A Life's Analysis

WHAT CAUSED ANNELIESE'S POSSESSION?

We do not know for certain what caused Anneliese's possession. Anneliese lead a normal life and there was never the slightest suspicion of her involvement in anything which could have precipitated her condition. One possible cause of her possession is as follows:

In 1947 Anna had a relationship with a man who worked at her father's sawmill. From this relationship, Martha was born on May 2, 1948. Josef and Anna subsequently met and married in 1950. Martha's father also married around this time. Martha's father's wife may have been jealous of Anna's marital and financial good fortune and may have initiated a curse on Josef and Anna's first born, Anneliese. Some people thought that it was more than a coincidence that Fleishmann had a daughter named Martha. A curse initiated by this woman is certainly a possibility. The majority of exorcists agree that many possessions are initiated by a curse. Often, during exorcisms the demons state that they entered as a result of a curse. In this case, the demons stated that a curse was initiated by a woman from Anna's village. In spite of this, all possessions occur only when permitted by God. It is our opinion that the cause of Anneliese's possession will remain a mystery. One can safely say, the demons wanted to possess Anneliese and God permitted this for her sanctification and the salvation of souls.

WHAT CAUSED ANNELIESE'S DEATH?

Based on her scientific research in the field of Anthropology, Dr. Felicitas D. Goodman believed that all religious influences are processed bio-chemically in the brain. In the case of a negative trance, or possession, the positive influences of the exorcism prayers are also processed in the brain. It was Dr. Goodman's opinion that the Tegretol may have impeded or stopped the benefits or positive influences of these prayers. Father Alt shares Dr. Goodman's thoughts in this regard.

In cases of possession, there are those who believe that medication should not be taken at all. It is our opinion that in Anneliese's case Tegretol was not the cause of her death. Starvation was clearly the primary cause of death. This obviously begs the question of why she stopped eating. For the believer in possession, the reason was the influence of the demons not allowing Anneliese to eat. For non-believers, the cause was mental illness. For those close to Anneliese, the action of the demons was a contributing cause to her death. The fact that Anneliese was diagnosed with circulatory problems by two physicians, and that Tegretol affects the blood, suggests that these factors along with physical exhaustion cannot be ruled out as possible factors contributing to Anneliese's death.

Father Alt offered three possible causes or contributing factors to Anneliese's death. One was physical or medical and two were spiritual. Firstly, Tegretol may have been a contributing factor as it may have affected the amount of oxygen in Anneliese's blood. Secondly, after Anneliese died, Father Alt went over the taped sessions thoroughly and came across a comment of the demons which stated "We are allowed to kill Anneliese." The two priests had not noticed these words at the time. For periods of time, the demons deprived Anneliese of food, drink and sleep and compelled her to over exert herself physically. In addition, Lucifer stated on October 28, 1975: "I will strangle the snotnose. I will do that next summer." Thirdly, there is the element of expiation. Anneliese had offered her sufferings to God for priests, the youth and her country. This was something she wanted to do and did so voluntarily. Anneliese was clearly and lucidly aware that her frightful struggles with the powers of evil would help others be saved. In February 1976, Anneliese told Father Alt that she had no more energy and was too tired to go on. Father Alt suggested that she think of what God wanted of her. Perhaps later there would be a situation where she could not go on. Anneliese then said that she wanted to do what God's will was for her. In April, when Anneliese stayed a week in Ettleben, she stated "I know now what will happen, I know that this coming summer will be hard and terrible and I know I will not survive. No one can tell me anything different. I will not survive." [62]

Since August 1975, Anneliese for periods of time, was not permitted to eat. In addition to being deprived of food, she often had very little sleep. In early May 1976, when she was permitted to eat, she couldn't keep the food down. At various times, while deprived of food and sleep, she was compelled to make countless genuflections which left her physically spent.

In dealing with this predominantly spiritual case, we should not forget that the Blessed Virgin Mary told Anneliese that people should expiate for the youth, for priests, and the fatherland. So many souls end up in hell because no one expiates and prays for them. The Blessed Virgin Mary then asked if Anneliese would be willing to offer her sufferings for the youth, the priests, and her country.

COULD ANNELIESE'S DEATH BEEN AVOIDED?

A spiritual problem can only be treated with a spiritual remedy. If a person is possessed by a demon, only prayer can expel it. Medical science is unable to treat such a case. Anneliese, from a medical point of view, would be considered a chronic case. If Anneliese had not been a religious person and had never been under the care of the priests, she probably would have spent most of her time back and forth between her home and a hospital. Her life would have alternated between long stays in the hospital and periods of time at home with her parents. After months or years (if the problem would have persisted in the same way), the probable result would have been her death. Whenever there are cases like this, people will demand medical attention, not realizing that the same outcome may result even while under the care of a doctor.

In spite of the foregoing, when Anneliese's physical condition began to seriously deteriorate in June 1976, those attending to Anneliese should have sought medical help. Even though the cause may be demonic, the effects were physical. With regard to her physical condition, a physician should have been consulted. If, or when, there was physical improvement, the exorcism prayers would be continued at such time. There were many factors as to why this action was not taken. Several of these factors were as follows: Anneliese, after years of multiple visits to doctors, believed that medical treatment was of no benefit to her. She had a deep fear of being sent to the mental institution at Lohr and made those close to her promise not to seek medical attention on her behalf. In August 1975, Anneliese had lost weight stating that she was not allowed to eat. She subsequently began to eat and put on weight. In June 1976, those close to her were anxiously waiting for July to arrive, as Anneliese had stated that there would be a resolution to her condition by July 1976. Obviously, those caring for Anneliese at the time of her death did not believe that she would die before the success of the exorcism.

A decision to send Anneliese to a hospital would have meant sending her to a psychiatric ward. This would result in separation from her family, priests and all religious activity, perhaps for months. Anneliese feared deeply being sent to such an institution and being at the mercy of a psychiatric doctor who might diagnose her insane. Anneliese and her family were opposed to testing those waters.

They had faith, and their faith would not be without payment.

From Anneliese's spiritual notes:

"You will pass all of your tests,
But you will be called upon to undergo tests of a different kind.
I will give you my grace.
You will be faithful till death."

FATHER ALT'S COMMENTARIES

The following two commentaries by Father Ernst Alt appear in the book *Anneliese Michel und ihre Damonen*, written by Felicitas D. Goodman, 2004 and are herein translated into English with permission from the publisher Christiana-Verlag CH-8260 Stein Am Rhein/Schweiz.

10 Years Later

The present book of Professor Dr. Felicitas D. Goodman is a precise, authentic and scientifically grounded presentation of the possession of Anneliese Michel – known as "the Klingenberg case." Nothing need be added to the book.

With these lines, I do not want to comment on the work of the cultural anthropologist Felicitas D. Goodman. It is my intention, ten years later, to present my personal thoughts and experiences in response to the request of the publisher, Christiana-Verlags. I am conscious of the fact that I will not meet with general approval. Nevertheless, after long consideration and hesitation, I could not decline the request of the publisher. Indeed, on closer consideration, I feel bound in conscience to point out essential points of the faith in the Klingenberg case over which I ought not to be silent after having gone into the countryside ten years ago.

I would like principally to indicate two dimensions of the case and their consequences which opened up to me and all those who took part, as we were forced to come to terms with the possession of Anneliese Michel:

First of all, with the dimension of Hell that is brought about when the creature wants to be like God. Satan desired this and still does. We all desire it, more or less, in every sin. And then the dimension of the divine work of salvation of Jesus, the Son of God became man, a dimension that continues until today in all the sacraments and ecclesiastical actions of the Catholic Church.

The Klingenberg case was for all those involved, a breathtaking experience. Someone on the outside cannot possibly appreciate this experience. Man's imagination is stretched past the limit when it comes to demonic possession.

The audio tapes that were recorded with the understanding of the possessed

(Anneliese Michel), give only an incomplete picture – and these cannot be listened to for long. What those who took part experienced is of such an intimate nature that it is not possible to communicate it. It was in the truest sense, "existential," i.e., something embracing the whole person.

The Klingenberg case, through the campaign of the mass media, was able to reach the public in a way never before experienced in such cases. Without exaggeration, one can say that the devil and demonic possession was vigorously discussed in all the lands of Europe and in the USA as a consequence of the Klingenberg case. Even if now the mass media no longer reports on this case, it remains relevant in the realm of theology and cultural anthropology and in some areas of society and in the realm of jurisprudence.

For someone who has the care of souls, demonic possession will always remain relevant, for he stands at the service of the Church, to whom the commission of Christ was given: Drive the demons out! In pastoral care it will always remain relevant since it entails the advancement of the Kingdom of God which is always to the detriment of the Kingdom of Darkness. In the name of Jesus, salvation was given to us. In the name of Jesus, Satan and his followers must depart. In the name of the crucified and risen God-man Jesus Christ!

The relevance of the Klingenberg case amazes anyone who knows the case, when he looks over the religious and social development of the last decade: Since 1975, the year in which the exorcisms were prayed in Klingenberg, and in which 6 demons gave their names (Lucifer, Judas, Cain, Nero, Hitler, and Fleischmann), Satanism is leaving the fearful vestiges of a victory parade through Germany. Since this time, the dismantling of the Church's' influence in public life seems to have been accomplished. Blasphemy in film and on television is called freedom of speech. Religious sensibilities are damaged even in the most sensitive areas. No one steps in to hinder this. Hardly a man of the Church wants to know about it! The seduction of youth has reached its height and produces its fruit: drug abuse, youth gangs, moral decadence and the demise of all Christian teaching in public. Terrorism and abortion show the bloody tracks of the one who was "a murderer from the beginning." Spirits is spreading even into small villages. Black masses are no longer a concealed rarity. The truths of the Faith are watered down by influential theologians. Faith is relativized and human freedom absolutized. But if the truths of the faith are no longer permitted to be true, and the freedom of man must not be limited in any way, then man will fall into the abyss of the creature who wanted to be like God, who "is called Satan and seduces the whole world" (Rev. 12:9).

After the journalists of all the papers for years had expressed outrage, the attitude of these same journalists was more than surprising, since previously they had given the appearance that they were bound to the truth. This attitude was revealing. Truth was left by the wayside. The "Klingenberg Show" was turned off. No one wanted anything to do with the conclusions of Prof. Goodman's book, for they would not be conclusions that touched merely on personal matters. This is surely an interesting case for cultural anthropology. We will definitely keep an eye out for future developments.

With regard to demonic possession, we are dealing with an essential truth of the faith. It is not a skirmish about trivialities. One truth stands above all others: Jesus Christ is Lord! In His name salvation is given to us. In His name we are redeemed. In His name we are to drive out the demons. In His name even the weakest servant of the Church is granted divine power in the struggle with the Kingdom of Darkness.

Jesus is the Son of God! Jesus is the Son of Mary. Jesus is present in all the sacraments. Those who took part in the Klingenberg case could say with Peter: "You are the Messiah! You are the Son of God" (Mt. 16:16)! Only with this confession of faith can one prevail against the gates of Hell.

Once in a while there arose in the believing observer a quiet rejoicing: It is true! It is all true! Jesus lives. He is truly among us… all the arrows of the demonic attacks are directed against the Son of God. The demons had to acknowledge him. They had to acknowledge him in a way reminiscent of the biblical scene: "We know who you are. You are the Messiah" (cf. Lk. 8:28, Mk. 1:24, Mk. 3:12). Nevertheless, they sought in their blind rage to attack the Son of God. They will always seek, in any way possible, to confuse or destroy the faith of those who believe. Yet, for all that, Satan wishes to become like God.

In the fullness of faith, those who took part in the Klingenberg case experienced the exorcisms as unrenouncable weapons, as a reality without which the Church in the course of her history would have never survived and in the future, regardless of all Hielseuphorie ("salvation euphoria") will not survive. Whoever altogether denies Satan, must of necessity also deny exorcisms. Because Satan exists, and today more than ever openly works with logical consistency, it is impossible from the point of view of the faith that exorcism be done away with. That would be a satanic triumph. In its shortest form the exorcism reads –and this is very biblical – "I command you, unclean spirit, as a servant of the Church, in the power of the crucified and risen Lord Jesus Christ, depart"! No need for modernization here.

What power and what role falls to the exorcist, Tatjana Goritschewa has described in her book *To Speak About God is Dangerous* as follows: "Father Anthony is a well-known exorcist all over Russia. He is thin, small and all gray haired. But he is not at all an old monk, not yet 60 years old. Out of the whole country the possessed and the insane come to the monastery, also simple people who are sick. It is interesting to note that, in day to day life these insane and possessed people cannot be distinguished from other men. In the monastery however, both sides of man are revealed, the best that is in him, as well as the worst. For the most part these are unfortunate, unhappy women. There are also men, but fewer. In the world many of them feel a constant, unbearable, oppressive weight. This feeling drives them to seek liberation in the monastery. Sometimes one hears loud howling and screaming during the liturgy in the monastery of Petschorskei; some roar like beasts, others throw themselves repeatedly on the ground, and others still belt out blasphemies in anger. It is not easy to lead such a screaming person to communion. A couple of men hold her with all the strength at their command. Again and again I have been amazed at the complete calm of the priest who is giving out communion. He works as "one who has authority", like a doctor, like a conqueror. After the reception of the holy gifts, those who were screaming before usually become quiet, their faces become relaxed and gentle, many cry silently".

A priest can only exercise his priestly ministry if he lives and acts with and for Christ. He is commissioned to spread the Kingdom of God. The extension of the Kingdom of God does not take place in some anonymous place; it presses upon the Kingdom of Darkness. An unbridgeable chasm opens up between these two kingdoms. In between there does not exist the smallest strip of "neutral territory". God's claim on us is too absolute. The depravity of Satan is too great.

Those who took part in the Klingenberg case were able to experience that the Kingdom of God is indeed threatened, but that it cannot be overcome by the Kingdom of Darkness. "For I am sure that neither death, nor life, nor angels, not principalities, not things present, nor things to come, nor powers, nor height, nor depth, nor anything else in all creation will be able to separate us from the love of God in Christ Jesus our Lord" (Rm. 8:38–39).

Nevertheless, there remains the threat to each individual who through his own fault can turn himself over to the Kingdom of Darkness and in that way loose his eternal goal. The reality of demonic possession speaks for itself. These demons gave eloquent testimony as they screamed for hours on end: "We are damned for all eternity"! The Kingdom of God does not know some neutral alternative. The only alternative is Hell. To speak here of a threatening message (Drohbotschaft) which does not correspond to the Gospel (Frohbotschaft) is wholly senseless, for we are dealing with a reality of our faith that is so and was not proclaimed otherwise by Jesus. If one plays down the assertion about eternal damnation, then one must also play down Jesus' death on the cross. Perhaps then, Christ's death on the cross was only a political accident.

For us all there remains the confession of Peter: "You are the Messiah. You are the Son of God" (Mt. 16:16). That means: a living faith has consequences for all that we do or fail to do.

The proper attitude with respect to the Son of God is an attitude of adoration. "When they saw him, they fell down and worshipped" (cf. Mt. 2:11): this was the great human accomplishment of the Wiseman out of the East. The power of God in the name of Jesus, the effect of the ministers of the Church in this name, the living God, His presence in all the sacraments, the faithfulness of God to all our prayers: these were all inextinguishable, powerful and comforting experiences.

In parallel to these experiences came also the experience of the power of Mary the Mother of God over the demons. With this power of Mary some of the truths of the faith became clear; truths which one as a priest and theologian well "knew", but which never inspired our life of faith.... We believe in the Immaculate Conception. The content of this truth of the faith became understandable when the demon announced himself. Gnashing his teeth he had to confess to have been cast into the abyss of Hell on account of his own fault; everything could have been different. At this moment all those who were taking part recognized what it means to say that Mary, the Mother of God, was conceived without original sin and that during her life, also remained without personal guilt. The guilt of Adam took on a fearful meaning, he who "wanted to be like God". No man can free another man from such guilt. But that is what Jesus did on the cross.

We experienced the particular favor of God which was bestowed on Mary, who chose her to be the Mother of God, which prepared Mary in a unique and great way. In this way the creature Mary was united in a most intimate way with the Triune God. Mary believed with the purest faith. Her hope was the most confident and trusting. Her love was the greatest love of a creature that has ever been shown to the Father and to the Son (who was also her Son) and to the Holy Spirit. The uniqueness of her being communicated itself to all the actions of her person: her freedom was exclusively a freedom for God. Her free actions had as their first goal, to adore the almighty God in love. She was the first adorer of God after the fall of Adam, the first adorer of the human race, from which there shall never arise another creature who can adore God in a purer fashion. In Mary there is united the deepest humility with the greatest obedience. No man was ever or could ever be more dedicated to God than she was. We were permitted to experience Mary as the first among those who believe and as a model for all the faithful. She was the way along which God came to us. She is the way along which we can go to Jesus – without a detour. There will never be another person who, for all these reasons, is as opposed to Satan as Mary. There will also never be a creature who has and will have such power against Satan. We were able to experience what the verse means: "She will crush your head" (Gen. 3:15)

Mary and Satan constitute the greatest opposition that there is between creatures. This opposition will remain irreconcilable. Mary will guarantee the truth of the crucified and risen Lord. Mary will stand up for the divinity of her Son – and hence also for the need to adore Him. Mary will stand up for His holy presence in all the sacraments, especially for the presence of God in the sacrament of the Altar.

It would be the epitome of a lack of logic, if the purest creature of God, the first of the redeemed, were not so totally for God and against Satan. In all the apparitions of Mary, even if they are designated as private, essentially nothing else is said. Her admonition is always an admonition to penance, conversion, prayer and fasting. It is always her most absolute demand to do the one and most important thing: to love God, to serve and adore Him, in order thereby to spread the Kingdom of God among and around ourselves. The more the light of God shines, so much more will the Kingdom of Darkness be pushed back and destroyed.

On the other hand, it will always be the case that the Kingdom of Darkness will always battle against the Kingdom of God and especially against Mary and her heel – i.e., her Son. But she will be the conqueress in all the battles of God. "She will crush your head"! Mary was for us in the fearful struggle of the Klingenberg exorcism, hope and comfort. I believe that I cannot remain silent on this point.

A similar experience was the experience of the effect of the holy angels. We are easily prone to represent the angels as little naked cherubs on our altar decorations and the crowns of our pillars. Furthermore one hears of the idea that, yes, angels do exist, but far away in some unreal region; that one can believe in such things, but is not obliged to do so and that surely it isn't the fashion to do so…Perhaps angels exist, but they are in any case not important for our life. We were able to experience the opposite.

Angels are pure spirits, created without a body. They were created for the glorification of the Triune God. They were created to be messengers of God's gracious love for us. They were created for the sake of creation's order and to gather it in at the end of time; created also, moreover, in order to lead men to their eternal goal.

We were able to experience that they also, as creatures, had to make a decision. They decided for God under the banner of St. Michael whose name means: "Who is like God." But not all the angels decided in favor of God. Many separated themselves from God, because they themselves wanted to rule, to be like God, because they, filled with pride and disobedience, no longer wanted to adore the Most High. Because it was made with such freedom and understanding, in this decision against God, there existed – I have to use the expression once again – no neutral ground in which one merely "wants to be different and act differently from the others." In such a decision against God, made with an understanding and freedom of the spiritual nature of the angel that is unimaginable to us, there arose the immeasurable distance from God and the inversion of all values – like that of faith, hope, love and adoration of God. That is how the Kingdom of Darkness originates. There the creature reigns who has lost his purpose and missed his eternal goal – without the least hope of recovering the smallest part of his former condition. It is perfectly logical then that there reigns an irreconcilable opposition between the good angels and the demons. Not only opposition but also hostility. The name of Michael is really nothing more than a battle cry which decided the life of the angels: spiritual creatures in the perfection of their being in the vision of God, standing before His throne, ready to execute the will of the Most High. They also stand in the service of God when they serve man, who is a pilgrim on the way. Their service guides men to the essential completion of their lives, which, likewise, can only consist in the adoration and glorification of God.

We were able to experience the power of the angels who stood by us. We were able to recognize with gratitude how the fatherly goodness of God inclined itself to us men in the services rendered by the holy angels. With howling and gnashing of teeth, the power of the angels was attested to by all the demons. One was forced to say: "You all should at the present time, honor you guardian angels more, since the power of Hell has grown to be so great". We all know that. Now we ought to get serious about veneration to the holy angels. About this also, I must not remain silent.

From these experiences, all of those who took part in Klingenberg were changed. Anneliese Michel consciously experienced all this as no one else did. She was not mentally ill. She not only registered all this, but was wide awake in her faith. It was for this reason that she insistently begged the help of the Church and exorcism. Her alert faith and the guidance of Heaven finally called her forth to bear her possession as expiation and in the end – of this I am certain – to throw her life on the scales of justice. As hard as it may sound to many: Is that not the logical conclusion when we are dealing with the advancement of the Kingdom of God at the expense of the Kingdom of Darkness?!

To get serious about conversion, that was the interior demand that was directed to us all. It is the age old call to repentance that urges us at all times. This truth about freedom, about man's intellect and will, will never change. We must concentrate all the powers of our souls in free acts of decision, so as to serve the Triune God.

The Klingenberg case was, for those who experienced it up close, a sign which stood as an immense warning in their lives and in these times. Its relevance will never pass. If the possession had remained concealed, it would have been a sign only for the small circle of those who took part. But half the world spoke about this case of possession. Science has concerned itself with it. The meaning of Klingenberg is greater. It has fallen to me still, in all humility, to point out the warning which was directed to all who have heard about this and discussed it. I do not think that I should be silent any longer.

In Klingenberg, the power and machinations of Satan and his cohorts and companions were made visible. Through this it became evident, that, all those are taken in by myths, who say that the devil does not exist. This experience with the power and machinations of Satan and the horrifying consequences for those who fail to reach their eternal goal, corresponds even in details with the pronouncements of Scripture and the teaching and experience of the Church. The Klingenberg case took place at a time in which Satan and Hell are vigorously denied. There has occurred simultaneously in our times, a falling away from the faith, greater than any in the history of Christianity. The divine Sonship of Jesus Christ is denied, the sacraments are made into mere signs, the living and all-present God is deliberately ignored and overlooked. Sin is excused. One negative development follows upon another. The complete loosening of religious bonds in marriage and the family, in education and public life, in politics and science is showing itself: divorce, abortions in the millions, euthanasia, gene manipulation, the leading astray of youth, etc., … I do not need to repeat myself.

But how has Germany recognized the sign that was planted in Klingenberg? According to a poll of a well-known institute in Germany, 31% believe in Heaven (USA 80%), and 14% in Hell (USA 66 %), 18% believe in the devil (USA 66%). I ask myself whether it was not like this in the past as well. I think about the Third Reich that I experienced as a child. Germany believed a Fuhrer, who in turn made the German people believe in themselves such that "with the German people the world will be made whole." My childhood was stamped by the horror of nights of bombing, the flight of low flying, strafing planes, the anxiety and prayer for our father who was in Stalingrad. We did as we saw others do, stood erect, raised our right arms and cried out (to the great distress of our mother) "Heil Hitler." Today there is a burning recognition: it was demonic. The Father of Lies was everywhere. Millions were dead.

Many came to their senses, but I think only to the degree that they saw this time as a mistake… not more. It is a great mistake, if this time is only seen as a "mistake." It is a mistake of the millennium, if we do not see in this Reich, the Reich of Satan – at least in hindsight. I am of the opinion that a reparation (without hard German currency) must be given: Germany should with this experience, warn the world about the Kingdom of Darkness.

It is still terrible today to watch documentaries where millions stand there and raise their right arm to honor the Fuhrer…Have they honored God and bent the right knee to Him? Have they at least learned in hindsight, as a reparation for the seduction of a whole generation? Have they dropped to their knees in adoration? How many have turned to this alternative and come to recognize the other alternative as satanic? With all the energy expended on reconstruction what could have been accomplished with regard to a moral and Christian reconstruction! Until today this reparation is still missing. The addiction to material things, the disintegration happening in many different areas, the increase in a wave of anti-God and anti-Christian sentiment is a proof that Christian and Catholic Germany has not learned... In Klingenberg there was a language spoken by the demons, which was clear and unequivocal. We do not need their exact words. It is sufficient to know about their existence and their hidden workings. In Klingenberg they were forced to show themselves to their own harm. In concluding, I cannot remain silent about certain connections with things that took place in Klingenberg which I believe are meaningful. I believe there were connections to be seen which clearly pointed to the fact that the Kingdom of Darkness was working in Germany during the so called Third Reich in a way that has never been recognized. I think I can state that the Kingdom of Darkness perhaps in a more powerful way will again spread in Germany. There is no other way to explain what is happening today.

All of Germany spoke about Klingenberg and the possession of Anneliese Michel. We were confronted by a storm of indignation, since the journalists were saying: That is impossible. The Psychologists were saying: Devils are products of an overactive imagination. The judges were saying: Anneliese was not possessed. She was mentally ill. Many were happy about this "good news." Life could go on. The case was solved.

Is there no one to acknowledge that it is a wonderful thing to serve God and His Kingdom? Does anyone recognize that it is the highest and most beautiful thing to adore the Triune God? Is there no one to recognize, that the intercession and help of the Mother of God can bring us to Jesus without any detour, that we can unite ourselves to her adoration? Is there anyone to recognize, that it is possible for us to fight for the Kingdom of God with the help of the holy angels – with the cry of St. Michael: "Who is like God?" Is there no one who will acknowledge that by these means, we can put an end to the present threat to our lives, our people and the whole world? Or is the young woman Anneliese Michel to remain alone in the fight against the Kingdom of Darkness? Are we to learn nothing from her possession? Is her life and death, whose anniversary we celebrate on July 1, 1986, to be no sign for us? Or are we just a clever nation full of cowards? Or a gifted nation, that has failed until now to understand its gifts, to the detriment of the European nations, with millions of dead? What ought we to think?

Do not raise your arm full of enthusiasm to a false Fuhrer! Do not grasp after materialism! Do not believe and ruin yourselves with half-truths! Do not give in to the pressure of the mass media! What then?

Bend your knee and adore the high God in a spirit of truth and love... That is the most important and holiest thing a man can do. It is something we must all do; all those who know about the possession of Anneliese Michel. One needs no organization, for ten people in every parish of Germany to get together, united with the first adorer of God, Mary, united with all the angels in the service which befits all creatures; united with them and under their leadership.

Ten in every parish. It could, however, also be a hundred.

After everything I experienced, I cannot be silent. I cannot say that Germany and the Church in Germany are not threatened. I cannot say that demons are a product of an overactive imagination! I cannot say there is no Hell. I cannot say that Anneliese Michel was mentally ill! I know that these are grave errors. But I must call ones attention to the most high Lord, to Mary, the first and most worthy adorer of God. I must point to the angels and their service to us… I know that the Triune God is honored and adored too little. I know that this and the sins of many people make possible the spread of the Kingdom of Darkness with such force as we experience at present.

The only alternative is: To adore the Triune God in the deepest reverence, along with Mary and all the angels and saints. In this way the Kingdom of God will grow and the Kingdom of Satan will be destroyed. That is the call that rings down the centuries. The message by which alone salvation comes to us. The relevant message, directed to us at this time, in the warning sign of the possession of Anneliese Michel from Klingenberg. If we, the whole of Germany, if Europe and the world would recognize this, that would be our salvation.

Ernst Alt

30 Years Later

2nd Commentary of Father Ernst Alt

I came to know Anneliese Michel in September of the year 1973. I had no idea that out of this encounter, the Klingenberg case would develop. I had no idea what this encounter would mean for my life. I recognize, as a fortuitous event (that is, the Providence of God), that the noted cultural anthropologist Professor Dr. Felicitas D. Goodman, who was altogether unknown by us, introduced herself to us and after a scientific investigation, finally wrote the present book about the events surrounding Anneliese Michel.

In the present, unabridged, new edition of this book, the publisher Christiana-Verlag, again confronts us with the truth about the Klingenberg case, i.e., with a scientific, accurate description and meaning of this case. Thanks are due to Christiana-Verlag for this venture in today's Church and our times.

A great media interest in the years 1976-1978 dragged our names like some kind of noxious mud – cultural mud – into the public light. Interest has in the following years abated. It remained, however, a potentially explosive topic, especially with people who have taken leave of the devil.

However, also in other circles of the Church, some didn't know exactly how one should handle the Klingenberg case. The fact of an officially sanctioned conviction always spoke against this case and is always brought forward as the principle argument for those who are opposed. In this statement I would like to consider a couple of important incidents that could very well lead to a different judgment of the case.

Since the above-mentioned media campaign, every year my name is dragged through the mud a few times. There are lies, falsifications and fabrications. Those who know better are dismissed. Investigations are undertaken that do not deserve the name. Some individuals with important names thought they were able to pass judgment on us. They knew none of those who took part, neither Father Arnold Renz, the parents, the sisters of Anneliese, nor myself. There were no telephone calls, no exchange of letters, no statements made on our part. But there was a condemnation, a so-called judgment with an official stamp of approval. They knew it all. This was all written down and made public as an interdisciplinary investigation commissioned by the German Bishop's conference.

I have often asked myself whether I should get upset about the brazen impudence of the thing or over its ridiculous scientific pretensions. Our names and our honor were repeatedly stomped in the mud. From high representatives of the Church to "snotty nose school children" (Walter Nigg), everyone knows that there is no devil and no such thing as possession, and with certainty, Anneliese Michel was not possessed but psychotic, sick.

In these 30 years I have, as opportunity has afforded me, avoided publicity. If I nevertheless announce myself after this long time, then the purpose is to present once again to an audience with even greater interest, the truth about the life and death of Anneliese Michel in a couple of incidents that others would like to conceal.

As her spiritual director, which I was from 1973 to 1975, I cannot allow that her terrible possession and her conscious acceptance of this as expiation which both Father Renz and I have established, be passed over as if it were some "theological accident." Anneliese Michel was possessed. All the priests who took part, Rev. Ferdinand Habiger, Rev. Karl Roth, Rev. Eduard Herrmann, and the expert on cases of exorcism, Rev. Adolf Rodewyk, S.J., were of this conviction. It was for us all a terrible and terrifying conviction. It became evident that with great probability, this possession came about by means of a curse, when Anneliese was yet in her mother's womb. As her spiritual director, I can say with certainty that Anneliese did not experience a possession of expiation in the sense of a possession like that of Marie des Vallees. The latter, as can be shown, offered herself in expiation in order to become possessed. She wanted in this way to save many souls from Hell. Marie des Vallees was a zealous and prized counselor of St. John Eudes.

Anneliese Michel recognized more and more, that her possession had a meaning not only for herself. She never invited this possession, it was also not "offered" to her by me, as some persons in a nasty calumny felt compelled to say. The case of Anneliese Michel was tested over a two year period. Finally all the priests who knew about the case, including the Bishop of Wurzburg, could do nothing else except begin the prayers of exorcism.

Anneliese was clear thinking and made clear judgments. There is no reason to doubt her decision to want to offer herself in expiation. She had, on the one hand, locutions and was comforted from Heaven, and on the other, she was strengthened and called upon in her willingness to offer herself in expiation. Her attitude of expiation can surely only be understood when one keeps these facts in mind. From this there emerges a deep, inner binding with Christ.

In February of 1976 I had a longer conversation with her in which she spoke about this interior attitude and that she wanted to offer expiation so that not so many souls would go to Hell. At almost the same time Father Renz recorded a conversation with her on tape where she said the same thing. At the beginning of May in 1976, I once again had a conversation with her in which she communicated to me: "I know what will happen to me now. I cannot be deceived any more." That corresponds exactly to another statement of hers: "It will become very bad again in the summer. Then I will have no more energy. I won't be able to survive." She recognized by this time, that her life would be demanded of her. She consented to this, of this I am certain. In this way we are to understand the expiatory offering of Anneliese Michel.

In the present book, Prof. Goodman presents the scientific results of her study of this exceptional religious state. She was able to confirm her methods in subsequent investigations. To this day this investigation and its results are deliberately overlooked by all the critics of Klingenberg. Can or will no one begin anything? Anneliese's consumption of medicines is likewise overlooked. It is nowhere recorded that these dangerous medicines were never examined by means of blood tests administered at regular intervals. Did someone make a mistake?

Dr. Richard Roth was consulted by me 3½ weeks before the death of Anneliese. One can read about the facts in Dr. Goodman's book. He made before the court two sworn and one unsworn statements that did not correspond to the truth. It was persistently concealed that a couple of weeks before the close of the trial, Dr. Roth was present at the conversation between Prof. Dr. Alfred Lungerhausen, Dr. Gerd Klaus Kohler, attorney Marianne Thora, attorney Frithjof Lipinski, Fr. Arnold Renz and myself.

He knew about everything perfectly well and attention was called to his role. As he made his statement before the court, I pointed out his lies to my attorney. She whispered to me: "Please be quiet. Dr. Roth is dangerous." So one could not put aside the accusation of perjury before the court. Proceedings were taken against him that were turned down. None of us were heard on this matter. *Anneliese Michel and Her Demons* is a book that cannot be read without emotion. The life and death of this young woman should at least be taken seriously by the Church. This book is also a presentation and document of the theological inability to deal with Satan and possession, Heaven and Hell. A young man said to me at the time of the appearance of the book in 1981: "This book tells the truth. When a person reads it, he must change his life. But most people don't want to do that and for that reason they will persecute you all." I have experienced it. Could we not also define the being and workings of the Church: The entrance of the baptized and confirmed into the Kingdom of God that they might also fight for this Kingdom against the Kingdom of Darkness? All the holy Apostles, martyrs and confessors have joined in this battle and have converted peoples and freed them from the yoke of Satan.

The command reads: "Drive the demons out" (Mt. 10:8)! Are we better or holier if we do not do it? And if we do not do it, what will happen to the Church and the world?! Is that an explanation for the present state of the Church and the world?

WORDS of the DEMONS

SATAN'S ANSWERS TO THE EXORCIST

The following words of the demons were compiled in the German book Anneliese Michel und die Aussagen der Damonen, written by Kasper Bullinger (Druck und Verlag: A. Ruhland, Rudolf-Diesel-Strasse 5- 84503 Altotting Bestell- nr.035). The book "Satan's Answers to the Exorcist" which contains the words of the demons (in English) was published by Fr. Adolf Faroni, SDB.

"By an inscrutable plan of God, Anneliese was possessed by demons from birth to death. She suffered till the end of her life. In spite of this continuous hellish torture, she kept on praying, going to mass, receiving the sacraments and saying the rosary throughout her life. She lived a most holy life and offered her life that souls may not fall into hell.

How many souls did she save with this suffering? This was God's way for her to save souls, and very many of them. God has his ways to which we have to bow reverently and humbly. What God permits, is always within His love, though, sometimes, it is hard for us to understand it."

(excerpt from forward by Fr. Adolf Faroni)

LUCIFER
1. "I am damned because I did not want to serve the Lord, even though I am a creature."
2. "I was in heaven and precisely in the choir of the one who is on the table" (the Archangel St. Michael).
Exorcist: "You could be among the cherubs!" Answer: "Yes, and I was."
3. "I am, now, the highest down there. St. Michael hurled me there. Now I cannot hurt him any longer, but the whole hell belongs to me."
4. "I want to conquer the earth for myself. In the meantime, I make a rich booty. I am filling up my kingdom. I take whatever I can take, I must convince you of this."

5. "Do you know why I fight so much? Because I was hurled down due to man."
6. "The majority have abandoned the Nazarene. How foolish! Those still faithful are a small flock."
7. "I never keep my promises."
8. "I am still the cause of enmity between one another...I am the devil!"
9. "I am bound to say even more. If that one did not oppress me so much! The Dame (Blessed Virgin) has trampled upon my head."
10. "I tell the truth if she compels me."
11. "I took Judas with me! He is always at my service. He is damned. He could have saved himself, but he has not followed the Nazarene."
12. "The Nazarene forgives always, if....that one (Blessed Virgin) often told it to him, that he had to amend himself."
Exorcist: "Would he do it again?" Answer: "No, never."
13. "Judas had many followers!"
14. "Among us there is no repentance, forever! Never rest. Rest and peace are up there."
15. "Do you know what a burning fire is there below?"
16. "Among us there is no obedience! This exists only up there."
17. "There is no return from there! Never, for all eternity! No one returns from there! There is no love, among us, there is only hatred. We have no peace, never. We fight one another. We too want to go up there!"
18. "The enemies of the Church belong to us."
19. "Pride brings men to ruin."
20. "When the world ends, we shall continue. Then things will become much worse. O, if you had an idea of how things stand there below! The visionary children of Fatima have seen it. If you had an idea as to how things stand down there, you would be on your knees day and night at... (tabernacle). I had to say it because the High Lady compels me to."

JUDAS
1. He repeats three times: "I am damned for eternity! You careless people, if you could just imagine what it is to be damned for eternity! I am damned!"
2. "I hung myself, because I was in despair and I had betrayed Him."
Exorcist: "Why have you betrayed Him?" Judas: "Because I needed the money."
3. "I do not want to come out (of Anneliese) where can I go?"
4. "Because of that one (Lucifer), I am in the hole. That dog has pulled me down."
5. "The Nazarene died for this society. But I take enough from them every day! The majority do not believe."
6. "I am the father of lies. I lie, as if compelled to do so. But that One compelled me to tell this to you (the truth)."
7. "I will not come out of the girl, down there, the torment is too great."
8. "There are not two truths: The truth is one, then we try with lies. Truth is up there."
9. "I will not come out of the girl. Down there, it is too tormenting."
10. "Also the other is now beside me, the one who was hanging on the cross near Him. He refuses to give his name."
11. "We shall fight for every soul."
12. "We want to come out of hell."

NERO
1. "I am the third of the covenant. I too am hidden down there."
2. "I have killed Christians and besides I have lived a dissolute life."

Due to novels and movies, Nero often appears in our subconscious to some as a literary figure rather than a historical figure. We must not forget that such a person lived and ruled Rome between 54 and 68 AD. He was responsible for the death of his mother and one of his wives. He persecuted Christians and under his reign St. Peter was crucified and St. Paul was beheaded.

CAIN
1. "I have killed my brother. I am burning."

HITLER
1. "I have killed so many. I have done away with the crucifixes, and now I am damned."
2. "Men are so beastly stupid! They believe that after death all is finished. But life goes on, either up or down."

FLEISCHMANN
1. "I am the sixth of the covenant, and precisely a damned priest. I was a parish priest at Ettleben. I am damned. It is horrible down there. Judas has pulled me down here."
2. "I kept faithful to Judas."
3. "I am damned because I fulfilled my duties very badly."
4. "When one is damned, his task is to be the ruin of other souls."
5. "I am eternally damned. The sufferings are frightful and most grave."
6. "I have killed one person, and I had women."

Exorcist: "Why have you done it?"

Fleischmann: "Because my duty was so heavy! I prayed too little. I was always in a hurry to finish my sacred duties. Now, I am down there languishing for eternity."

7. "You priest, if you knew of what power you are vested! But you do not want to have it!"
8. "I am to be pitied: but now we can no longer wish (there is no more remedy)."

STATEMENTS OF DEMONS REGARDING ANNELIESE

September 9, 1975

Lucifer: "The pretentious one is obsessed. This is our work. She cannot take an examination. I will take care of it. I have had enough with this snotnose. I have tormented her long enough, at least for six years. I have tormented her so much that she has cracked. I will not leave her, not even if you move a thousand times your paw (he intended to say to Father Renz that he would not come out even though he gave him a thousand blessings). The snotnose is cursed. I will not leave her free. I will not get out alone. And we are so many inside her!"

Judas: "The other one who was on the cross near Him, on the left side, is hiding himself within her too."

Exorcist: "Tell me your name!"

Judas: "I will not do it. Both of us, in fact, are damned. And I will not get out alone."
Exorcist: "What is stronger, you or the crucifix?"
Judas: "Then I go into something else, there are still many here." Fight among the demons: "No one wants to get out. That other one who hides within her, not even he wishes to get out, hence I too do not want to quit. You get out! I will not. This one (Anneliese) has in fact read Barbara Weigand and she also went to Schippach, this cursed snotnose, this dirty wicked woman and also this individual, who is before me (the exorcist). This snotty girl cannot take any exams, I know that too. The cursed slut is obsessed and this is the result of our work. (new discussion about getting out of her). No one wants to go out first. They insult one another with dirty words like "sow, we have taken her: we will not go out! I have to get out soon: yes, but there are still many inside her, to give you trouble (to the exorcist)."
Exorcist: "Are you seven?"
Judas: "No, six!"
Lucifer: "I want full possession of the snotnose, in whom I have already lived for quite a time. I want to possess her, only for myself. The dirty water of San Damiano and the snotnose drinks it all day, filthy! But today no one believes it! The snotnose, this cursed witch does also mumble a lot (prays the rosary). We are going to torment her for a time still, this cursed slut. The one who has sold (Judas) should be the first to leave. Oh, she did not hang herself. It was that other (Blessed Virgin Mary) who prevented her from doing so, in fact, she is under her protection! She was cursed from the beginning. She was cursed before her birth! The snotnose is ours! You have to pray much more. By order of that one (Virgin Mary) they should still recite... rosary or else, we cannot come out. This affair will last for at least half a year still. By order of that lady, people should fast."

October 1, 1975

Lucifer: "The other one of that village, where the curse took place, was an envious woman: that woman of your mother's village."

October 6, 1975

Lucifer: "I have to say something. Therefore the snotnose has to pay for it."
Exorcist: "You have to get out of her!"
Lucifer: "I don't want out yet, because I have to say many things still!"
Judas: "No, we will not come out! Even if you recite that thing (exorcism prayers) a thousand times, we will not come out! Yes, yes, I have cursed her: in fact I am still inside her. I will stay for some time within her. She belongs to the one below. I have cursed her."
Father Rodewyk (to Judas): "Now you too can get away. Anneliese, by now, cannot stand any more, physically as well."
Judas: "She must bear a little longer still because she was cursed and because he (her guardian angel) is near her, or else she would already have hung herself!"
Lucifer (to Father Alt): "In fact, the snotnose was cursed. She belongs to us. The one from.... cursed her. She is no longer alive."
Exorcist: "Is she down with you?"
Lucifer: "No! The snotnose, yes, she belongs to us, she is ours, we have pinched her."

October 10, 1975

Judas: "First, let us torment the woman still!"
Exorcist: "How long still?"
Judas: "When I have said everything, then I will get out."
Nero: "The snotnose was cursed by a woman. I will come out soon. There are many of the kind of the snotnose."

October 13, 1975

"The guardian angel of the snotnose is here. Before I leave, I will tell: we are six...."

October 15, 1975

Lucifer: "The snotnose blurt out everything! Now she also receives suggestions from that one (Blessed Virgin Mary). Of the kind of the snotnose there are still so many. They were taken to the neurotic clinics. The one from... (Mrs. N...) Is not crazy, no! She exaggerates, yes, but crazy, no! He (the Savior) allows this, yes, but the snotnose is saving many souls with this. We are five (in addition to him): Judas, Nero, Cain, and Hitler."

October 17, 1975

Lucifer: "I will deal with the snotnose until she cracks. She cannot even realize this, because we have stopped it from above. That she faints continuously is our doing too."
Exorcist: "Why do you treat Anneliese this way?"
Lucifer: "Because we have to leave her soon, so the pigs (people) believed at once. I had permission. We have to come out this month. I am crouched inside her because she was cursed by a woman of... The lady. It was really she who ordered it for me to do it! It happened in 1951! Because she was a resentful woman. Yes we have perverted her. The snotnose was often in bed and sick. We have done this too. We are the cause of many illnesses! But this no one sees it now. Pray for the sick. Set one's life according to Him... (Christ): then nothing can get lost! During the examination I have confused her. We tired her out. We are so interested in possessing her!"

October 20, 1975

Lucifer: "We will get out in the month of that one (Virgin Mary), her... (month of Mary, October). Judas Iscariot will be the first to leave. Then the others will follow him. I will be the last to leave, in October. We shall all leave in October and we shall go somewhere else. In Lohr (neurological clinic) there are more of us hidden there. There, one goes neither forward nor backward. I would be much happier if I had the snotnose there, at Lohr. With this it will be shown the power we have, and what power we have on the intellect and on the will of man. The snotnose has never spoken of it even though it seemed so (during her crisis). In her examination to qualify for the university she wrote almost nothing. During the examination of the German language we have blown in her ears for hours telling her that she was damned. The first manifestation was in the tenth grade. Judas did it. We were the cause of all her ailments. She got them from us: tuberculosis, infection in her head, sickness in her throat. We have continuously caused them to the end. We did not bring her to suicide. To be among the damned, this was our most wicked intent, the worst for her. With this you can fancy what power we have on the intellect and on the will of man. We have suggested to her that He (the Savior) said that she was damned. The last day of October we shall leave her all of a sudden. And how pleased you will be! You have the power of expelling us. The great majority do not make use of it. And these are those who are most dear to me. The cursed slut will again be able to take her examinations. She knows nothing, because she has not put anything in her head. But that one, up there, wishes her to take her exams! The one who cursed the snotnose is a lady... She is not damned and has fooled us. I wished her to be with us so willingly! However, unfortunately, what a pity, I have to leave soon. The snotnose continues saying everything. Do you know why she was not brought to the clinic? Because through her everything should have been revealed so that the bishop would be able to know everything."

October 22, 1975

Lucifer: "We shall soon leave her. The one up there is expelling us. We are damned eternally. We also want to go up there. We do not want to go out. We shall still torment the snotnose. She is still under the protection of the one up there (Virgin Mary). On October 31, 1975, at night, we shall leave her. They have to be here!"

October 24, 1975

Fleischmann: "Today we are six, one more, a damned priest. On October 31, 1975, I have to leave. You will have a sign next time. I have not the duty to give it. The woman... has cursed her. Now she is crushed, down at the bottom. She has to pray for that woman. The cursed slut has to give us her soul, but we, however, have not brought her to this point. She goes too often to the church. She has followed the Nazarene. But we will make things difficult for her. Those too have prayed too much. Grandmother brought her to church. She was six years old. Grandmother has pulled down her bed almost every day. I was within her since the beginning. The others came afterwards. There are quite a number of people who curse other people...Then we enter once more. The nephew of the chaplain Roth died (Siegfried). He too is high above and continues to look down and the snotnose knows it well. Siegfried is in heaven. We too could be there. We monkeys! He has already come to visit the snotnose. He is twenty years of age. Barbara Weigand and her mother (Oma Michel) are here too. Martha, Anneliese's sister is here as well. They are all together. We have to get out soon, on October 31, 1975."

October 27, 1975

Lucifer: "The snotnose has never been separated from the Church (never in mortal sin). This is inconceivable!"
Fleischmann: "I have a message from the one who cursed the snotnose. You have to pray for her. She is down there, in the deepest purgatory."

October 28, 1975

Lucifer: "I will strangle the snotnose. I will do that next summer. The dirty slut has begun to notice that we do not give her respite. Do you think that we shall vanish? Yes, I will come out. That's why we can still torment people."

October 31, 1975

Present: Blessed Virgin Mary, St. Joseph, Barbara Weigand, Siegfried, Brother Conrad and Guardian Angel. They come out revealing their names and reasons for their damnation. The joy of all those involved feeling that each of the six demons have been expelled is short lived.

November 3, 1975

Judas: "We shall not go out. Our business will take some time more. We just deceived you. We will not go out. Today the dirty slut went to mass. She should not go to church. Stop with that thing, (pointing to the exorcist). After all, it is useless. We should not come out as yet. We are going to torment the snotnose for some time more. She does not know anything, and cannot take the examinations. Last Friday, we exhausted the snotnose."

November 8, 1975

Judas: "I am eternally damned. I am here again, ready for some time. Do not always call me by name!"
Present: Lucifer, Cain, Hitler, Judas, Nero, Fleischmann … a total of ten demons. "By order of the High Dame, be patient."

November 10, 1975

Judas rages again because Anneliese goes to church, and because frequent communion was introduced by Pope Pius X.

November 23, 1975

Judas: "The filthy slut went to church again today. We hate this!"
Exorcist: "Do those who do not go to church please you?"
Judas: "If they knew what is in store for them by so doing!"
Exorcist: "Could you tell us something on this matter?"
Judas: "I am not so stupid! But it will fair them extremely bad."
Present: Blessed Virgin Mary, St. Joseph, Siegfried, Theresa Neumann, Father Goirdano, Pope Pius X, grandmother and other ancestors, the Guardian Angel and the Archangel Gabriel.
Judas: "Hurry up, one cannot stand it any longer! But we too here are very many. The affair will last for some time yet, before we leave."

December 12, 1975

Lucifer: "If that one goes once more (to Communion), I will break her into pieces. I will spit out that thing (the host). And to make things worse, she also kneels down, that stupid sow!"

December 14, 1975

Judas: "I won't get out. The reason is because we are not compelled to. This affair will go on still for some time, not for a long time, however."
Exorcist: "How many are you?"
Judas: "This is not your business."
Exorcist: "Tell me your name!"
Exorcist: "Judas!"

December 19, 1975

Exorcist: "Where is Fleischmann?"
Judas: "He is away but he may still come back... And there are still many more here, and you know absolutely nothing. We too want to go up there (heaven). We are damned, eternally! Out! Out! We wish to come out of the snotnose. We cannot bear staying any longer. That filthy slut stays the whole day in the church. We are damned! Damned!"
Exorcist: "Then come out!"
Judas: "We cannot, because He does not allow us. The One up there! That One does not want it! He wants us to remain still some time... We want to get out from that one, who goes to Communion and she goes every day! We wish to come out, out, out! And she even kneels down. We wish to come out, but the one up there does not allow us!"
Exorcist: "Why does he not allow you?"
Judas: "Ha! Because, ha! Because? We wish to come out, out, out! Stop praying! We are damned, damned, damned! We want to come out, we are damned, damned! (on the word damned on the tape there is a dreadful emphasis). Do you know what that one knew at the examination! It is inconceivable! She deserves a mark of three. She will infallibly pass the next examination. It is He, up there who has permitted it...."
Exorcist: "If you recite a Hail Mary, hell will shake and the demons will flee."
Judas: "Yes this is true."

January 6, 1976

Exorcist: "Why can you not come out?"
Judas: "We do not know the reason! We have taken the robber at the left side."

January 23, 1976

Judas: "We cannot torment those who have a place in heaven. In this century there will be as many Saints as never before. However, many come to us too, and people do not believe this! Everybody thinks that they are okay and provide every comfort

for themselves. Are they really all so stupid? O, if they knew! But then it will be too late! Then there will be no return! The dirty slut that cursed one, that stupid sow...."
Exorcist: "Is she not doing what you wish?"
Judas: "No! But sometimes yes. All do this as well as those who will take their place above. He permits it, so that they do not become proud. Why should I say this? It is also written in the Scriptures."
Exorcist: "Should you cooperate to foster the love of God?"
Judas: "Yes, so it is! And this is the most frightful thing."
Exorcist: "Why do you remain still here so long?"
Judas: "To work in the dirty slut. I will break her totally."
Exorcist: "Go to the desert!"
Judas: "This is an expression not too bad! Damned! Damned!"

January 26, 1976

Exorcist: "Why don't you go away?'
Judas: "We cannot!"

February 1, 1976

Judas: "Next week, the dirty slut will not eat. She has to fast, that stupid slut! We still want to torment her, and it is also useful to fast. After all, she will not die of starvation! For the exams she can eat. But she knows really nothing, really nothing! This last week she has learned absolutely nothing, really nothing! If she had our advice, she should not have studied. We have always worked against her, we have always been present. But the One above does it. He does it step by step. O, if someone is under our power, then that one will dance like us, we play the music, just as the dirty slut should dance. If we wish, we can! She cannot do otherwise, she must do it, even if she does not want a thousand times, she must do it all the same, because she is a human being. I have accomplices."
Exorcist: "Who usually helps you most, and more often?"
Judas: "I jump to her face!"
Exorcist: "And what profit do you draw in tormenting Anneliese?"
Judas: "It is our amusement! There is only wickedness and torment within us. We wish to come out!"
Exorcist: "Then get out if you wish it."
Judas: "It is useless, we have lost her! O, terror! She cannot guess it! Yes, here too a fire is burning, but worse, much wars (in hell)."
Exorcist: "Do you like carnival?"
Judas: "Yes, we love it."

February 8, 1976

While Father was imposing a scapular on Anneliese and commanding the evil spirits to leave her at once.
Judas answered: "We cannot, so soon, still not so soon. It will be in summer."

February 13, 1976

Judas: (to the exorcist) "We are damned! Your mother is now, out of purgatory and we are crushed down there."
Exorcist: "You have to leave!"
Judas: "We cannot! Only when the High Dame and He (Savior) permit it. It will not be too long from now."
Exorcist: "Do you know when you have to leave?"
Judas: "Yes! High Dame!"
Exorcist: "Who said that we should still continue?"
Judas: "That one! (Through Anneliese, she points at the statue of the Blessed Virgin Mary)."
Exorcist: "Then we must continue. The Most Holy Virgin Mary commands it to you."
Judas: "I say nothing! No, no! Shame! I am Judas, I say nothing! The room of the snotnose is almost destroyed by the fire. Do not be so impertinent! I have blown (fire in the room). That was a nice amusement! The stupid sow, that one should not have blessed candles burning always. Unfortunately she got a bit dirty with soot."
Exorcist: "Who has helped, if not the whole omnipotence from above?"

February 16, 1976

Exorcist: "Who are you?"
Judas: "We are damned, you...."
Exorcist: "Why do you get so angry if we show you the statue of St. Michael the Archangel?"
Judas: "Because I like to do so. I can't stand him. Out, out, out you rapacious!"
Exorcist: "You ought to let Anneliese go to Communion."
Judas: "No!"
Exorcist: "Did you understand?"
Judas: "Yes!"

February 20, 1976

Judas: "We wish to get out."
Exorcist: "Then why do you not get out?"
Judas: "We wish to get out of hell and from that one (Anneliese), out of both of them."

February 23, 1976

Judas: "We are damned, damned, damned! We want to get out!"
Exorcist: "Why are you damned? Why have you kissed the Lord?"
Judas: "Because I fell into despair!"
Exorcist: "You cannot stay here long!"
Judas: "If you know so much, there is no need for me to say more!"
Exorcist: "Will it be within this week?"
Judas: "No, I shall not tell it!"

Exorcist: "When can Anneliese go to Communion?"
Judas: "The snotnose cannot go, only when the One who was crucified on the cross will allow her to go to Communion. During Mardigras (carnival) we are set free. We still have to deal with the snotnose (language indecently abusive), do you understand? Yes, tonight I will torment her as she deserves!"
Exorcist: "I forbid you to do so!"
Judas: "No, because I will trample upon the stupid sow. She had no peace for the whole night! It is Mardigras. The High Dame needs reparation and substitution for the others who will dance with me the whole night. Yes, I am after her..."
Exorcist: "She is under the protection of the Virgin Mary."
Judas: "Yes, but she is a person. She will not make noise externally the thing could go also otherwise..."
Exorcist: "Who are you?"
Judas: "We are damned, we are damned!"

February 29, 1976: No response.

OTHER THINGS SAID BY DEMONS REGARDING EXORCIST AND OTHER TOPICS

September 29, 1975:

1. Judas (Father Renz): "You are consecrated: It is terrible. I do not take you. You are under the protection of the (Mother of God)."
2. "No, you must call me by name!"
3. "I know you have been in China and there you have offended me greatly. You snatched souls from me! I do not understand you (while he laughs) but I understand you very well also in Chinese!"
4. "The one from Frankfurt (Father Rodewyk) has expelled me already several times, but now, he can no longer do so because he is too old."
5. "That other one (Gertraud, Anneliese's sister) goes down there to Portugal and preaches of that one (Virgin Mary) and speaks of the apparitions in 1917. No one believes in them today. That one is taking too many from me, the snotnose, that stupid, that cursed. Now she is soon coming."
6. "Roswitha should not go so often to church, because that is hateful to me since men are saved with prayers."

October 22, 1975 (Lucifer)

1. "Saul (St. Paul) has persecuted the Christians: but then he has snatched souls from me."
2. "That parish priest of Ar's (St. John Vianny, patron saint of parish priests) against whom we have fought so much, we could have done even more, if we had been free. But we can act only as far as the length of our chains."

October 27, 1975

1. Lucifer (referring to Bishop Rodolf Graber of Ratisbon): "It is quite a time that

Bishop Graber is a thorn in my eye."

January 23, 1976

Father Renz (to Lucifer): "You are responsible for heresies, for example those of Kung!"
Lucifer: "Yes, and we have still more."
Father Renz: "And Bishop Lefebvre?"
Lucifer: "Ha! That one! But they do not believe in him. What a pity!"
Father Renz: "Who says: what a pity?"
Lucifer: "Not I!"

DEMONS SPEAKS ABOUT CONDITIONS OF THE CHURCH

September 29, 1975: (Judas to Father Renz)

1. "That thing that you wear (cassock and collar), the great majority do not wear it any longer. These modernists are the result of my work and they already belong to me."
2. "They no longer obey the Pope in Rome. It is the one in Rome who still keeps the Church going."
3. "This Encyclical [Humanae Vitae] is also with no result, it is useless."
4. "The religious in the monasteries watch television and do not pray enough, do not kneel down and they extend their paws (he intends to say that they receive Communion in the hand)."
5. "This is done by everyone; all do the same, from Bishop to the parish priest. Also the... at... allow them to stand and gives it to them on their paws."

October 1, 1975: (Judas to Father Renz)

1. "Today, no one believes any longer in the Immaculate Conception. For this reason they are crushed, where I too am crushed."
2. "The parish priests are all the same, beastly stupid. They are all pinched by me. In fact I am the traitor, and the majority is exactly like me. In fact, they too betray the Nazirite."
3. "The one down there (the Pope), he alone still keeps the Church standing. The others do not follow him, do not obey. Everybody wants to be modern."
4. "The parish priests pray too little, they sit in front of that one... instead of adoring it (the Blessed Sacrament). I already have an entire multitude in my trailer. If they believed in the one down there (the Pope) they would behave better. All act independently, and more, they also believe they are clever."
5. "The rosary, they do not think it is modern. Even the parish priest does not recite it. He recites the Rosary once a week, and he believes to have worked a miracle having done so. Every day! No! I say nothing! How I wish the One up there did not exist! (Mother of God)"
6. "The Church? At present, the great part believes that it is only a community. The modernists are killing it evermore. We are hard at work at this, so that it may be drawn, and we through much poison into the Church, so that it will be drawn.

By now, those who believe in the Church and are faithful and believe in her are very few."

7. "The ugly book (pointed out with the usual indecent abusive language, that is the Dutch Catechism) they have written is cursed. What is written in the Our Father and do not lead us into temptation, it is forged. It is written in James 1-13. (God cannot be tempted and He does not tempt any one.) It should read, Do not let us fall into temptation but deliver us from the evil one."

8. "Many believe that after life, everything is finished. They are very many, and they live accordingly, because they do not pray any longer."

9. "Sins reach Heaven: but the thing will not last long. The one of 1917 (Our Lady of Fatima) said it. But only few have listened to her. Death, tribulations and famine, O yes, they will come again. The One up there does not keep looking down any longer! But fortunately no one believes in it any longer! So then, we can take so many more with us!"

10. "The films are bad and television is not better."

October 7, 1975

"The rails (of Communion) are no longer there, in all churches."

October 17, 1975

"No one speaks any longer of us, especially the Reverend Parish priests."

October 10, 1975

1. "I particularly know Kung (theologian, disciplined by the Church) of Tubinga quite well. The Bishops are so foolish as to believe the theologians rather than the Pope."

2. "This is the month of the Rosary but very few recite it, because the parish priests think it's not modern. They are so foolish! If they knew its importance! It is a strong weapon against Satan and against us. I have to say it, unfortunately many do not believe in it."

3. Nero: "The Dutch bishops are heretics. They have become unfaithful to the Pope!" (Members of the Dutch synod asked Rome to suppress celibacy, grant permission for married priests, and admit women to the priesthood. The Church's position on these matters is clear).

4. "On Saturdays, it is good to be in bed and have more rest! I like it! One should pray day and night."

5. "The Catholics have the true doctrine and they run after the Protestants, like prostitutes! The Catholics give the doctrine of truth away to the pigs who eat it!"

6. "There in the synods, (language indecently abusive) they continue to deliberate. The bishops already know what they should do. There would be no need of synods if they followed the Pope. For them the Pope is foolish! They are those who let that thing (the host) be given in the hands!"

October 22, 1975 (Lucifer)

1. "The worst thing is this: that the doctrine is falsified in the Church!"
2. "You have the power to expel us, to make us come out! The majority do not care."
3. "Many do not go to church any longer. No one kneels down to the box (the Blessed Sacrament). And the Church is not doing well since the time it was founded. The churches are so modern! The Church adapts itself too easily to the world. The Nazarene and His Mother are now attacking! But now, the situation will not last much longer, it will burst soon."

October 27, 1975

Fleischmann:
1. "In ... they have snatched a Host. They presented themselves. They have extended their paws and went away. It was reduced to small particles, rather, more than one Host, four. And then they have sold them to one who is at my service! But they have not received much for this. Yes and how could such a thing happen? On the other hand this happens very often! Not only to x... there are still other masses. If the Bishops did not permit Communion in the hand, this would not have happened. Perhaps one has to attentive. But now, this will not go on for a long time, afterwards one will end up in a ditch. This is said by the High Dame."

Lucifer:
1. "Many particles are taken and desecrated, not by you, because it is difficult for you. This is our best amusement, to cause pain to the Nazarene and to His Mother. Many priests have an uneasy conscience! On one side they have to obey their bishop, and on the other side their conscience!"

January 23, 1976 (Judas)

"The new Creed is very different, totally different: Descended into the kingdom of death. Thus they deny hell! But if they knew, what beautiful flowers are down there, and they bloom for them! The parish priests too interpret it wrongly! One should say: He descended into Hell."

October 20, 1975 (Lucifer)

1. "Some no longer have any spark of faith: they belong to me!"
2. "The churches are empty! Few go there. They are in bad shape."
3. "Haag! This is a nice fool! If anyone believes in what he says, he fares very badly."
4. "Yes, the parish priests should say that I exist. Or else they will all go down! The Dame compels me always, because she wants to save the wicked people. However, not everything happens as she wishes, because she says too little in her messages."
5. "The candidates to the priesthood should pray. They should be formed in their own seminaries. They should not go to other universities."
6. "This is the worst: the falsification of the doctrine. The bishops should turn to Rome for enlightenment."

Nero
1. "One must show obedience to the Pope."
2. "The very reverend parish priests should preach from the pulpit what refers to me! People should be informed of it!"
3. "They should wear the clerical garb."
4. "The priests should be recognized as such."
5. "People should go to confession."
6. "The Catholic doctrine should be announced without falsification, especially the doctrine of the Eucharist and the Immaculate Conception."

October 14, 1975 (Fleischmann)

1. "The majority of people should go to the priest when they are sick. This is the command of the High Dame."
2. "You should pray very much, because the punishment will come very soon, so that not too many will come with us. Recite the rosary."
"Communion in the hand should be abolished. This is my work. The Bishop should now forbid Communion in the hand, if he had permitted it before."

At one point in time, two thirds of the Bishops were against introducing Communion in the hand. Pope John Paul II clearly did not endorse this even into the 1980's. When he came to Canada in 1984, he gave Holy Communion on the tongue only. Mother Teresa is also on record as not being in favor of receiving Communion on the hand. The primary reason for receiving Communion on the tongue was due to the danger of profanation and sacrileges. Receiving on the tongue also reduces possibility of particles of the Blessed Sacrament falling to the ground.

In light of the forgoing words of the demons regarding Holy Communion and Anneliese's personal views on same, here are some of the official norms of the Catholic Church as set out in Redemptionis Sacramentum.

It is the Priest celebrant's responsibility to minister Communion, perhaps assisted by other priests or Deacons; and he should not resume the Mass until after the Communion of the faithful is concluded. Only when there is a necessity may extraordinary ministers assist the Priest celebrant in accordance with the norm of law.

"The faithful should receive Communion kneeling or standing, as the Conference of Bishops will have determined," with its acts having received the recognitio of the Apostolic See. "However, if they receive Communion standing, it is recommended that they give due reverence before the reception of the Sacrament, as set forth in the same norms."

Although each of the faithful always has the right to receive Holy Communion on the tongue, at his or her choice, if any communicant should wish to receive the Sacrament in the hand, in areas where the Bishops' Conference with the recognitio of the Apostolic See has given permission, the sacred host is to be administered to him or her. However, special care should be taken to ensure that the host is consumed by the communicant in the presence of the minister, so that no one goes away carrying the Eucharist species in his hand. If there is a risk of profanation, then Holy Communion should not be given in the hand to the faithful.

Only out of true necessity is there to be recourse to the assistance of extraordinary ministers in the celebration of the Liturgy...

If there is usually present a sufficient number of sacred ministers for the distribution of Holy Communion, extraordinary ministers of Holy Communion may not be appointed. Indeed in such circumstances, those who may have already been appointed to this ministry should not exercise it. The practice of those Priests is reprobated who, even though present at the celebration, abstain from distributing Communion and hand this function over to laypersons.

October 10, 1975 (Nero)

1. "Yes, you should follow the message of Fatima!"
2. "The Encyclical Humanae Vitae is decisive, there is no other way! The whole Humanae Vitae!"
3. "If this is not done, there will be another punishment. You will all come to a wretched end, especially here in Europe."
4. "The rosary should be recited, or else it is the end!"

October 13, 1975 (Lucifer)

1. "Democracy in the Church is not necessarily the best way because obedience is buried. The parochial councils are also not the best thing! The parish priests should command. The priest's should act according to their conscience, but above all, they should move around with the clergymen. One should pray more to their Guardian Angel because the power of hell is now too great. Men should beg their Guardian Angels to assist them."

October 15, 1975

1. "Holy water should come back in the houses! Also the Crucifix should return to its place in the home."
2. "Priests should easily and ordinarily be recognized as such. If they moved around dressed with their own, we would not have so much power on the mob."
3. "By her order (Virgin Mary), the five holy wounds should be venerated in a special manner."
4. "The Holy Face should be venerated! This is commanded by the Nazarene because it is so much disfigured by men! For this reason it should be venerated."
5. "The medal of the Holy Face should be venerated. This is ordered by the One who has the power over heaven and hell. Also the image painted by Sister Faustina should be propagated (Divine Mercy). Where this image is, come many blessings, to our great ruin. He Himself has commanded us to tell it, the Nazarene and His Mother."
6. "The priests, too, should venerate the Holy Face. He wishes this earnestly. All the priests and all men should venerate the face of God."
7. "It is very important to pray to St. Joseph. Rather it is most important!"

October 27, 1975 (Fleischmann)

1. "No priest should marry! He is a priest forever. And with the religious, there is no difference! They should remain faithful to their vocation!"

October 24, 1975 (Lucifer)

1. "You should preach more. By order of the One up there, you should warn people of the danger of the world without God. They have abandoned the One in whom they can find peace."

October 10, 1975 (Lucifer)

1. "If the message of Fatima is not given due importance and Humanae Vitae respected, a new punishment will come."
2. "It won't last much longer. The chastisement is coming. That thing (the contents of the audio cassette) must beforehand be made public. Many will yet be saved. Above all she (the Mother of God) prepares everything. The warning is that which precedes the other (perhaps she refers to the chastisement).
Exorcist: "What is to be done? " Answer: "Kneel down and pray!"
3. "The guardian angels are day and night near you, behind you, so that you may follow the Savior. We follow you step by step. We are spirits. Today people do not believe in the guardian angels. They are my enemies. I hate them."

October 17, 1975 (Lucifer)

1. "We have also tormented Barbara Weigand enough."

October 22, 1975

1. "The Eucharistic covenant of love should be diffused. This is not done. I beg you to do it. All hell would be against it. I do not wish the love covenant because it snatches too many souls from us. The One they have nailed on the cross, the one Judas has betrayed, wishes the love covenant."

October 24, 1975

1. "Besides it was said by the One who has built the Church. But today they no longer believe in it. She was derided and despised. And yet, unfortunately, it is true. The writings of Barbara Weigand will soon be published. But I will not allow this to be done easily."

October 22, 1975

Father Renz: "Can we still save many souls with our prayers?"
Lucifer: "Yes! Also the hardened ones, but then penance is to be done, with sacrifices and with perseverance! Especially, you should adopt a way of living according to the Nazarene! Barbara Weigand has preached this enough. Also this she did not do

willingly. And yet she did it. There must be the will to correct and better oneself always!"

October 27, 1975 (Judas)

1. "But no one enters the covenant."

November 9, 1975

1. "The one from Schippach is the right one for the renewal (Barbara Weigand)."

January 22, 1976

1. "Lucifer is not pleased with that one (Anneliese) who has copied the writings of Weigand, and I too do not like it. It is certain that the powers of darkness will become more powerful. Also this is written inside, and this is true. And it is also true that men will occupy places which were left vacant up there, and that we can torment them. In this century there will be so many saints as never in the past. However, many also come down here with us, and people do not believe. They all believe that all is well with them and they provide every comfort for themselves. All of them are demons. If they knew! But then, when they realize it, it will be too late... then, no one will ever come back...!"
2. "Lucifer speaks of the poor souls (in purgatory). We cannot persecute the poor souls. They have the prospective and the hope of Heaven, and even if they should stay there till the last judgment, one day, they will come out!"

REGARDING ABORTION

October 10, 1975

Nero: "Abortion is homicide. It is always homicide no matter in what month it takes place. The soul of an embryo does not come to the presence of God. It goes to Heaven, but does not have the beatific vision because it has not been baptized."
Lucifer: "The unborn children can be baptized."

REGARDING MARIAN APPARITIONS

Lucifer: "She (Blessed Virgin Mary) would have so many places where she would be left alone. If you did not have that one over there, many of you would be with me! San Damiano... down there. I prevent people from praying down there, the mother of God is near and she distributes many graces to you. The apparitions at San Damiano and Montechiari are true. The Church did not approve them, but this is the fruit of our work."

VARIOUS COMMENTS

September 29, 1975 (Judas)

1. "People standing during Holy Communion. This pleases me more than kneeling. It is not necessary to be kneeling, I hate it. The parish priests make everyone stand and gives it on their paws. I do everything possible that no one be on his knees."

October 15, 1975

1. "We are very happy with the new reforms. We are most happy with these changes."
October 16, 1975

1. "The giving of Communion on the hand was my work."

October 20, 1975 (Lucifer)

1. "There are people who do not believe I exist. They are my dearest ones. I love Haag very much! He puts the world upside down!"
2. To Father Alt: "When you do not wear the priestly garb you are more pleasing to us. But the greatest part, do not use it at present and it pleases us immensely."

FROM THE SPIRITUAL NOTES OF ANNELIESE

1. The Lord wants obedience from me, because of this, I write: "Every sorrow, even a small one, bears much fruit, if united to My Passion."
2. The Savior wants that: "You will suffer much and you will atone from now on."
3. The Savior: "You will withstand all your trials. You will be called to bear other trials. I will give you my grace. You will be faithful till death."
4. "Pray without ceasing for your neighbor so they may reach the eternal motherland."
5. "Pray and offer much for my priests. I have shown you the greatness and dignity of every priest, so much so, that you were frightened. Keep in mind that even the unworthy priests are another Christ. To avoid judgment, do not judge anyone. Leave this task to me."

APPENDIX

San Damiano and Montechiari:

Due to the fact the demons who spoke through Anneliese mentioned two pilgrimage sites (San Damiano and Montechiari), we will provide a brief history of each alleged appearances of the Blessed Virgin Mary. The intent is not to give an opinion as to their authenticity.

San Damiano is a place of pilgrimage in the north of Italy near Piacenza. The story of the pilgrimages is connected with Rosa Buzzini. Rosa's doctor had strongly recommended a therapeutic abortion. Rosa firmly refused and had a difficult delivery. Her health gradually deteriorated. On September 24, 1961, Rosa was in the hospital, gravely ill with perforated peritonitis. As there was nothing they could do for her, she returned home where she resided with her Aunt Adele. Before noon on September 29, 1961, the feast of Saint Michael the archangel, a beautiful woman came to their door asking for a donation for candles for the sanctuary of Padre Pio. The visitor was seeking 500 liras, half of what they had borrowed. She gave the woman the 500 liras. The lady turned to Rosa who was in bed and asked if she believed in Padre Pio. She stated that she did. The lady then told her that she was to visit Padre Pio. They then prayed together five Our Fathers, five Hail Mary's and five Glory Be's, for Padre Pio's intentions. At this time the lady touched Rosa's wounds which closed instantaneously. Aunt Adele then to her surprise found Rosa doing the dishes. "I have been healed!" Rosa exclaimed. They believed it had been the Blessed Virgin Mary who had paid them a visit. Rosa returned to a normal life and went to mass each day.

In May 1962, Rosa went on a pilgrimage to San Giovanni Rotondo where Padre Pio resided. People came from all over the world to confess to the stigmatized priest. As Rosa was praying the rosary outside the church, she heard a voice calling: "Rosa, Rosa!" Rosa turned and saw the woman who had previously visited her. The lady asked, "Do you recognize me?" Rosa answered: "Yes you are the Madonna who healed me." The lady stated, "I am the Mother of Consolation, the Mother of the afflicted. Tell these words to San Damiano and to the professor who did not believe in your cure. After mass I shall lead you to Padre Pio." The lady then disappeared, and during Rosa's visit with Padre Pio, he told her she was to help the sick in their physical and spiritual needs for a period of two years.

Two years later, Rosa's Aunt Adele took sick and Padre Pio told her to go home and look after her. He also told her, she would live through a great event.

On October 16, 1964, Rosa heard a voice coming from the garden: "Come, come!" Thinking this was an illusion, she was afraid. "Come here, come here!" Rosa took her rosary and went out into the garden. Suddenly a beautiful cloud appeared and settled over a pear tree. Out of the cloud appeared the Blessed Virgin Mary. She smiled at Rosa and said: "My daughter, I come from afar. Tell the people, that all must pray, as Jesus can no longer carry His cross. You must help him carry it. I want everyone to be saved, good and bad alike. I am the Mother of Love, the Mother of you all. You are all my children. That is why I want all to be saved. If people do not pray, there will be great calamities. While you are alive, I shall appear here every Friday at lunchtime and give you messages which you are to pass on to the world." Rosa replied: "I am only a poor farmer. No one will believe me, they will imprison me." "Be not afraid," Our Lady replied. "I shall leave you a sign, this pear tree shall bloom!" At the moment Our Lady disappeared, the pear tree became covered with blossoms so profuse that the people could barely see any foliage. Despite autumn storms, the tree continued to bloom for three weeks. A well was later dug at Our Lady's request and many healings took place.

At San Damiano, many conversions have taken place. It has been claimed that there have been signs in the sun. Mama Rosa died on September 5, 1981. Since 1975, her health had steadily deteriorated and she had to be admitted to the hospital on several occasions. She received Holy Communion fifteen minutes before her death while surrounded by her children and grandchildren.

Montechiari

In the spring of 1947, while praying in the chapel of the local hospital in Montichiari in northern Italy, Pierina Gilli (a nurse) claimed to have seen an apparition of the Blessed Virgin Mary. Mary appeared with tears in her eyes. Pierina noticed three swords in her heart. The first sword symbolized the unworthy celebration of Holy Mass and Communion unworthily received; the second meant unfaithfulness to and giving up the vocation as a priest or a religious; and the third symbolized betrayal of the faith. Our Lady asked for Prayer, Sacrifice and Penance.

The second apparition took place on July 13, 1947. Mary appeared with three beautiful roses in place of the three swords. The white rose represented the spirit of prayer; the red rose, the spirit of sacrifice; and the yellow rose, the spirit of penance and conversion. She smiled and said: "I am the Mother of Jesus and the Mother of all. Our Lord sends me to bring a new Marian devotion to all religious orders and institutes, male and female, and to the priests of this world. I promise to protect those religious orders and institutes who will venerate me in this special way, increase their vocations, and achieve a greater striving for saintliness among the servants of God."

The apparitions continued with various messages with the seventh coming on December 8, 1947. While praying the rosary in the Basilica, Pierina called out: "O, Our Lady!" Mary said with a smile: "I am the Immaculate Conception. I am Mary, full of grace, Mother of My Divine Son Jesus Christ. Through my coming to Montichiari, I wish to be known as the Rosa Mystica." Two dramatic healings apparently took place at this time. Pierina withdrew to a convent where she served in the kitchen and waited 19 years for Our Lady to return on White Sunday (Sunday after Easter) April 17, 1966, as promised. Four apparitions took place: April 17, May 13, June 9, and August 6, 1966.

After the apparitions of Our Lady, Pierina withdrew from the public and was obedient to the Bishop who ordered her to remain silent.

THE EXORCISM OF EMILY ROSE

The movie *The Exorcism of Emily Rose* opened in theaters across North America in the summer of 2005. The film, directed by Scott Derrickson, is based in part on the life of Anneliese Michel. His objective was not just to make a scary movie, but to also provoke thought on the questions of: Does the spiritual realm exist? Is there a God? Is there a devil? The movie does a good job of depicting possession and exorcism. It also treats the cause of Anneliese's condition, in a balanced or neutral manner, leaving the viewer with a choice to make as to what really happened.

The German film *Requiem*, directed by Hans Christian Schmidt, was released in 2006. In spite of some positive attributes of this movie, if it was an attempt to evidence the actual life of Anneliese Michel, it does not do justice to Anneliese Michel as a person and treats her condition primarily from a medical and psychiatric perspective.

With regard to movies dealing with this subject, the movie *The Exorcist* (1973) should be mentioned. This film shows, in a correct and realistic way, the ritual part of exorcism. With regard to possession, signs of possession appear in the movie and are depicted to be as terrible as in real life. The film should however, be considered as a catalogue of everything that can happen during hundreds of exorcisms. Levitation, for example, is extremely rare and the majority of exorcists never witness it during their lifetime. In the end, after viewing many movies on possession and exorcism, we feel two films worth seeing are *The Exorcist* and *The Exorcism of Emily Rose*.

ACKNOWLEDGEMENTS

We would like to thank Father Robert for his patience and German translations of material and taped interviews. Belinda Gore for permission to quote various materials from Dr. Goodman's book and her ever gracious and prompt responses to any questions or requests. Christiana Verlag for permission to quote Father Alt's commentaries. Father Faroni for permission to quote from his book. Father Ernst Alt and a friend for their time and patience in answering questions. Peter Hein, Thea Hein and Anna Michel for their time in answering questions. Sonja and Alex for translations and visit with the Heins. Also thank you to Helge Cramer, Hadwig Munstermann, Marc Philippens, Bernd Ruhland, Martin Roth, Winfried Erb and family. Dr. Reg Hutchison, neurologist. Father Chris Sherren for editing comments. Mia Wuertz, Jenny Duersch and Agostinho Ouana for German interviews and translations. Father John Molina, Erica Stanley and Erica Gilligan for Spanish translations. Ted Pazdzierny for Polish translation. Carol Little for copy editing.

ABOUT THE AUTHORS

Jose Antonio Fortea Cucurull "Father Fortea"

Father Fortea was born in Barbastro (Huesca, Spain) on October 11, 1968. He lived in Barbastro until entering the University of Navarra, Spain, where he obtained a Bachelor's Degree in Theology. He was ordained deacon in January 9, 1994 and priest on July 3, 1994. He has always belonged to the Alcalá de Henares diocese, Spain. He obtained the Licenza Degree in Theology, in the field of History of the Church, in the Faculty of Theology of the Comillas Pontifical University. He defended his thesis of licenza entitled "Exorcism in the Present Age" under the direction of the Secretary of the Commission for the Doctrine of the Faith of the Conference of Catholic Bishops of Spain, in the year 1998. Some time later, he started taking care of cases related to demonic possession at the parish where he worked as a pastor. He worked in this ministry until he moved to Rome, where he doing his doctorate in Theology on the topic of exorcism.

He is a well known author in the field of demonology, demonic possession and exorcism. He travels around the world giving lectures on these topics.

Lawrence E. U. LeBlanc has a degree in Business Administration from Saint Francis Xavier University and co-owns and operates a business on Prince Edward Island, Canada where he resides with his wife and two children.

BIBLIOGRAPHY

Although several books have been written concerning this story, we have used *The Exorcism of Anneliese Michel* by Dr. Felicitas D. Goodman as a bibliographical basis for our citations.

1 Der Teufel is in Mir, by Uwe Wolff. Page 99
2 Der Teufel is in Mir, by Uwe Wolff. Page 100-101
3 The Exorcism of Anneliese Michel, by Dr. Felicitas D. Goodman, Doubleday& Company, Inc., Garden City, New York, 1981. Page 26
4 The Exorcism of Anneliese Michel, by Dr. Felicitas D. Goodman, Doubleday& Company, Inc., Garden City, New York, 1981. Page 32
5 The Exorcism of Anneliese Michel, by Dr. Felicitas D. Goodman, Doubleday& Company, Inc., Garden City, New York, 1981. Page 28.
6 Translated telephone conversation between Lawrence LeBlanc and Thea Hein, September 2006.
7 Interview of the author with Father Ernst Alt and Winfried Erb dated January 9, 2007.
8 The Exorcism of Anneliese Michel, by Dr. Felicitas D.Goodman, Doubleday& Company, Inc., Garden City, New York, 1981. Page 43-44.
9 The Exorcism of Anneliese Michel, by Dr. Felicitas D. Goodman, Doubleday& Company, Inc., Garden City, New York, 1981. Page 44-47.
10 Interview of the author with Father Ernst Alt and Winfried Erb dated January 9, 2007.
11 The Exorcism of Anneliese Michel, by Dr. Felicitas D. Goodman, Doubleday& Company, Inc., Garden City, New York 1981. Page 61-64.
12 The Exorcism of Anneliese Michel, by Dr. Felicitas D. Goodman, Doubleday&Company, Inc.,Garden City, New York 1981. Pages 73, 75 and 76.
13 The Exorcism of Anneliese Michel, by Dr. Felicitas D. Goodman, Doubleday& Company, Inc., Garden City, New York 1981. Page 72
14 The Exorcism of Anneliese Michel, by Dr. Felicitas D. Goodman, Doubleday& Company, Inc., Garden City, New York 1981. Page 77-78.
15 Egzorcyzmy Anneliese Michel a Polish documentary directed by Maciej Bodasinski, written by Maciej Bodasinski and Leszek Dokowicz 2007.
16 Interview of the author with Father Ernst Alt and Winfried Erb dated January

9, 2007.
17 Egzorcyzmy Anneliese Michel a Polish documentary directed by Maciej Bodasinski, written by Maciej Bodasinski and Leszek Dokowicz 2007.
18 Interview of the author with Father Ernst Alt and Winfried Erb dated January 9, 2007.
19 Egzorcyzmy Anneliese Michel a Polish documentary directed by Maciej Bodasinski, written by Maciej Bodasinski and Leszek Dokowicz 2007.
20. Translated telephone conversation of the author with Anna Michel, September 2006.
21 Egzorcyzmy Anneliese Michel a Polish documentary directed by Maciej Bodasinski, written by Maciej Bodasinski and Leszek Dokowicz 2007.
22 Interview of the author with Peter and Thea Hein January 8, 2007, Germany
23 Egzorcyzmy Anneliese Michel a Polish documentary directed by Maciej Bodasinski, written by Maciej Bodasinski and Leszek Dokowicz 2007.
24 The Exorcism of Anneliese Michel by Dr. Felicitas D. Goodman, Doubleday& Company, Inc., Garden City, New York 1981. Page 85.
25 Interview of the author with Father Ernst Alt and Winfried Erb dated January 9, 2007.
26 Der Teufel is in Mir by Uwe Wolff. The same was corroborated to author by Peter andThea Hein during interview dated January 8, 2007.
27 Interview of the author with Peter and Thea Hein January 8, 2007, Germany
28 Interview of the author with Peter and Thea Hein January 8, 2007, Germany
29 Interview of the author with Father Ernst Alt and Winfried Erb dated January 9, 2007.
30 The Exorcism of Anneliese Michel by Dr. Felicitas D. Goodman. Doubleday& Company, Inc., Garden City, New York 1981. Page 106-107
31 The Exorcism of Anneliese Michel, by Dr. Felicitas D. Goodman. Doubleday& Company, Inc., Garden City, New York 1981. Page 114
32 Interview of the author with Father Ernst Alt and Winfried Erb dated January 9, 2007.
33 Egzorcyzmy Anneliese Michel a Polish documentary directed by Maciej Bodasinski, written by Maciej Bodasinski and Leszek Dokowicz 2007.
34 The Exorcism of Anneliese Michel, by Dr. Felicitas D. Goodman. Doubleday& Company, Inc., Garden City, New York 1981. Page 137-138.
35 The Exorcism of Anneliese Michel, by Dr. Felicitas D. Goodman. Doubleday& Company, Inc., Garden City, New York 1981. Page 149-154.
36 The Exorcism of Anneliese Michel, by Dr. Felicitas D. Goodman. Doubleday& Company, Inc., Garden City, New York 1981. Page 160
37 Interview of the author with Father Ernst Alt and Winfried Erb dated January 9, 2007.
38 Egzorcyzmy Anneliese Michel a Polish documentary directed by Maciej Bodasinski, written by Maciej Bodasinski and Leszek Dokowicz 2007.
39 Der Teufel is in Mir, by Uwe Wolff. Page 283
40 Der Teufel is in Mir, by Uwe Wolff. Page 301
41 Egzorcyzmy Anneliese Michel a Polish documentary directed by Maciej Bodasinski, written by Maciej Bodasinski and Leszek Dokowicz 2007.
42 The Exorcism of Anneliese Michel, by Dr. Felicitas D. Goodman. Doubleday& Company, Inc., Garden City, New York 1981. Prologue xxi-xxii.

43 The Exorcism of Anneliese Michel, by Dr. Felicitas D. Goodman. Doubleday & Company, Inc., Garden City, New York 1981. Page 178

44 Translated telephone conversation of the author with Thea Hein, September 2006.

45 The Exorcism of Anneliese Michel, by Dr. Felicitas D. Goodman, Doubleday & Company, Inc., Garden City, New York 1981. Page 184-185.

46 Interview of the author with Peter and Thea Hein January 8, 2007, and with Father Ernst Alt and Winfried Erb dated January 9, 2007.

47 The Exorcism of Anneliese Michel, by Dr. Felicitas D. Goodman. Doubleday & Company, Inc., Garden City, New York 1981. Page 186

48 The Exorcism of Anneliese Michel, by Dr. Felicitas D. Goodman. Doubleday & Company, Inc., Garden City, New York 1981. Page 187-188.

49 The Exorcism of Anneliese Michel, by Dr. Felicitas D. Goodman. Doubleday & Company, Inc., Garden City, New York 1981. Page 188

50 The Exorcism of Anneliese Michel, by Dr. Felicitas D. Goodman, Doubleday & Company, Inc., Garden City, New York 1981. Page 14.

51 The Exorcism of Anneliese Michel, by Dr. Felicitas D. Goodman, Doubleday & Company, Inc., Garden City, New York 1981. Page 17-18.

52 The Exorcism of Anneliese Michel by Dr. Felicitas D. Goodman. Doubleday & Company, Inc., Garden City, New York 1981. Page 194

53. The Exorcism of Anneliese Michel by Dr. Felicitas D. Goodman. Doubleday & Company, Inc., Garden City, New York 1981. Page 197-198.

54 Von Wemding nach Klingenberg by Dr.Georg Siegmund, Christiana-Verlag Ch-8260 Stein Am Rhein/Schweiz.

55 Anneliese Michel und ihre Damonen, by Dr. Felicitas D. Goodman, Christiana-Verlag Ch-8260 Stein Am Rhein/Schweiz.

56 Interview of the author with Peter and Thea Hein January 8, 2007, Germany.

57 Inexplicable events examined, verified miracles, legal finding of facts, by Harald Grochtmann, 1988 (3rd edition) Unerklarliche Ereignisse, uberprufte Wunder und juristische Tatsachenfeststellung (Broschiert)

58 Inexplicable events examined, verified miracles, legal finding of facts, by Harald Grochtmann, 1988 (3rd edition) Unerklarliche Ereignisse, uberprufte Wunder und juristische Tatsachenfeststellung (Broschiert)

59 Inexplicable events examined, verified miracles, legal finding of facts, by Harald Grochtmann, 1988 (3rd edition) Unerklarliche Ereignisse, uberprufte Wunder und juristische Tatsachenfeststellung (Broschiert)

60 Inexplicable events examined, verified miracles, legal finding of facts, by Harald Grochtmann, 1988 (3rd edition) Unerklarliche Ereignisse, uberprufte Wunder und juristische Tatsachenfeststellung (Broschiert)

61 Der Teufel is in Mir, by Uwe Wolff. Page 300

62 Interview of the author with Father Ernst Alt and Winfried Erb dated January 9, 2007.

Printed in Great Britain
by Amazon